"How wonderful to meet my long-lost sisters from Tang Dynasty China. Their voices cross many hundreds of years and many thousands of miles to reach me. They speak to me of their struggle for recognition as women, of their love of the natural world, of their commitment to a spiritual path. They inspire me with both their courageous assertions of autonomy and their longings for connection. Big thanks to the translators for this great gift."

—Susan Moon, coeditor of *The Hidden Lamp: Stories from Twenty-Five Centuries of Awakened Women*

"This exquisite collection of poems by three Daoist women who lived during the Tang Dynasty is filled with beauty, surprise, the everyday, and the sublime. It is a book that will move and inspire, and one that we will return to again and again."

—Joan Halifax, author of *Being with Dying* and *Standing at the Edge*

"With *Yin Mountain,* translators Peter Levitt and Rebecca Nie invite us into the worlds of three exceptional Tang-era Daoist women poets. Redolent with imagery and metaphor, steeped in the familiar and the strange, the poems in this collection comfort and challenge as they dance between interpenetrating dualities of mind and body, love and loss, yearning and contentment, intimacy and distance. Savor these poems—in translation and the original Chinese characters—with the guidance of Levitt and Nie's contextualizing notes. Clouds and rain, silk and talons, dragon bells and hawk perches, wild moths and pebble friends—such things will never be the same after reading this book."

—Chenxing Han, author of *Be the Refuge: Raising the Voices of Asian American Buddhists*

"These beautiful translations reveal the spiritual depth of these powerful women's poetry, and take us deep inside the mysteries of Daoism's ancient goddess culture."

—Meredith McKinney, translator of *Gazing at the Moon: Buddhist Poems of Solitude*

"*Yin Mountain* is an easily accessible and reliable introduction to the lives and work of three enticing Daoist women poets of medieval China. These elegantly rendered poetic traces of their self-realization in the face of many of the same challenges we face today cannot but comfort and inspire."

—Stephen R. Bokenkamp, translator of *A Fourth-Century Daoist Family: The Zhen'gao, or Declarations of the Perfected, Volume 1*

"There is no better way to capture the primordial essence or spirit of things than through the breath of poetry. In *Yin Mountain*, Levitt and Nie bring to life through poetry the goddess culture not often acknowledged in Chinese Daoism. Here, three Daoist female poets are brought into the light where all can experience the passion of yin and the love and mysticism within it. This book is truly an added gem to the existing ancient teachings of priestesses, nuns, and goddesses around the world."

—Zenju Earthlyn Manuel, author of *The Shamanic Bones of Zen*

"The introduction of women poets from ancient China to Western audiences is itself an epoch-making endeavor. The brilliance of the translations in *Yin Mountain* and the elucidation of the background material are breathtaking."

—Kazuaki Tanahashi, cotranslator of *The Complete Cold Mountain: Poems of the Legendary Hermit Hanshan*

"Ever since Ezra Pound 'discovered' Chinese poetry for the English-speaking world, the strange and delicate allure of this subtle tradition has been part of our culture. After about a century of translation of important male poets, we can now see, in this beautifully translated volume by Peter Levitt and Rebecca Nie, the other side of the coin. *Yin Mountain* presents the works of three well-celebrated Daoist women: Li Ye, Xue Tao, and Yu Xuanji. With useful and succinct introductions to each poet and head notes to make appreciation of each poem fully accessible, Levitt and Nie's versions are lovely—in the fullest sense."

—Norman Fischer, author of *Nature, There Was a Clattering As . . .*, and *When You Greet Me I Bow*

"I always wondered what was on the other side of China's Poetry Mountain. Thanks to Levitt and Nie, now that I've become the guest of Daoist priestesses and courtesans, I have to ask myself whether I should let my friends know or keep this to myself."

—Red Pine, coeditor of *The Clouds Should Know Me by Now: Buddhist Poet Monks of China*

YIN MOUNTAIN

The Immortal Poetry
of Three Daoist Women

Li Ye 李冶
Xue Tao 薛濤
& Yu Xuanji 魚玄機

TRANSLATED BY

Peter Levitt & Rebecca Nie

SHAMBHALA

Shambhala Publications, Inc.
2129 13th Street
Boulder, Colorado 80302
www.shambhala.com

Cover art: Werner Forman Archive / HIP /
Art Resource, NY; sleepwalker / Shutterstock.com
Cover design: Kate E. White
Interior design: Lora Zorian

9 8 7 6 5 4 3 2 1

First Edition
Printed in the United States of America

Shambhala Publications makes every effort
to print on acid-free, recycled paper.
Shambhala Publications is distributed worldwide
by Penguin Random House, Inc., and its subsidiaries.

LIBRARY OF CONGRESS CATALOGING-IN-PUBLICATION DATA

Names: Levitt, Peter, translator. | Nie, Rebecca, translator. | Li, Ye,
active 8th century. Poems. Selections. | Li, Ye, active 8th century.
Poems. Selections. English. | Yu, Xuanji, 842–872. Poems. Selections. |
Yu, Xuanji, 842–872. Poems. Selections. English. | Xue, Tao, 768–831.
Poems. Selections. | Xue, Tao, 768–831. Poems. Selections. English.
Title: Yin Mountain: the immortal poetry of three Daoist women / Li Ye,
Xue Tao, and Yu Xuanji; translated by Peter Levitt and Rebecca Nie.
Description: First edition. | Boulder, Colorado: Shambhala [2022] |
Includes bibliographical references.
Identifiers: LCCN 2022010949 | ISBN 9781645471127 (trade paperback)
Subjects: LCSH: Chinese poetry—Tang dynasty, 618–907. | Chinese
poetry—Tang dynasty, 618–907—Translations into English. | Chinese
poetry—Women authors. | Chinese poetry—Women authors—
Translations into English. | LCGFT: Poetry.
Classification: LCC PL2658.E3 Y46 2022 | DDC 895.11/30809287—dc23/
eng/20220329 LC record available at https://lccn.loc.gov/2022010949

We dedicate this collection to our beloved daughters,
Sheba De Ponce and Selena Tara Nie,
and with deepest gratitude to our mothers,
the generations of women through
whose wombs we came,
and the millennia of unsung women
whose art, labor, and love
nourished life in all places and times.

CONTENTS

GUIDE TO PRONUNCIATION

The romanization of Chinese letters and words that appear to the left of the colons below is based on the Pinyin system. We have provided approximate English pronunciations to the right of the colon following each letter or word.

Letters
x: sh
c: ts
q: ch
zh: jh
z: tz

Important Names
Jiangxi: Ji-ang-she
Ruan: Roo-an
Xiakou: She-ah-ko
Xiao-Xiang: She-ow She-ang
Xie Ke: Sh-eh Kuh
Xue Tao: Shu-eh Tao (pronounce the *T* as in Tom)
Youjun: Yo-juin
Yu Xuanji: Yu Shu-an-ji
Zhong: Jhong

*Tang Daoist priestesses in their official vestments as found
in the seventh-century text* Daoist Code of Conduct.

PREFACE

Yin Mountain presents our translations of three female Daoist poets who lived and wrote during the Tang Dynasty, universally regarded as the "golden age," when classical Chinese poetry reached what many consider its most profound and sophisticated range of expression. While readers of poetry in translation from this extraordinary period may easily recognize the names of the male poets Du Fu, Li Bo (also known as Li Bai), Wang Wei, and the legendary hermit-poet Hanshan, the names of the Chinese women poets—and especially those for whom the principles and practices of the Dao were central—are hardly known at all.

Relying on the magnifying lenses of Daoism, naturalism, mysticism, diverse experiences of love, and the comings and goings of daily life as lived by these women, the poetry of Li Ye (ca. 732–784 C.E.), Xue Tao (ca. 758–832 C.E.), and Yu Xuanji (ca. 843–868 C.E.) weaves together plain but poignant and revealing speech with a compelling and inventive use of imagery that expresses their devotion to Daoist spiritual practices and, as well, the myths, legends, and traditions of goddess culture relevant to both Daoist understanding and Chinese culture during the Tang dynastic period in which they lived.

Readers may find it of interest that at this time, Daoist priestesses were considered demigoddesses. It's no wonder, then, that our poets sometimes relied on the legends and spirit of the goddess of erotic passion and intimate affairs said to reside in the clouds that drift above Wu Mountain. As poems related to the Goddess of Wu Mountain by Li Ye and Xue Tao make clear, locating the mysterious and unsayable Dao, which they considered their "original home," in a woman's sensuality is a powerful statement of the Daoist understanding at the time that among other essential attributes associated with the Daoist female principle known as *yin*, a woman's passion and physical, sensual nature is an embodiment of the Dao in female form. As such, it is meant to be explored, expressed, and praised as the source of life itself. As it says in the sixth chapter of the Dao De Jing,

> The Valley Spirit never dies.
> It is called the Mysterious Female.
> The gateway of this Mysterious Female
> is the source of heaven and earth.

But there is more, for this source and its spirit, ungraspable as they may be, were fundamental to many other poems that reveal not only the poets' spiritual practice and development but also their loves and losses, and an intertwining of personal and spiritual love in imagistic poetic expression four hundred years before the great Sufi poet Rumi wrote of the Beloved in poems of a similar nature. In addition, their connection to this source can be found in poems of correspondence with suitors, lovers, and other artists, and, importantly, in poems that express the painful struggles they faced as women, despite the undeniable fact that even during their lifetimes, starting when they were young, their extraordinary talents were recognized and admired.

Consider the case of Li Ye, for example. She was an ordained Daoist priestess whose poetic talent was noted in a significant manner by her father when she was just five years old. (It is said that he was so struck after hearing a particular poem of hers, spoken at that young age, that he remained shaken for quite some time.) As she entered her later years, her talent and reputation were so substantial that they led to the great honor of being summoned to the palace by the emperor to teach the royal entourage in residence, including the young women in the emperor's harem whom Li referred to in her knowing poetic way as "fragrant grasses."

To gain a further sense of the heart and mind of this extraordinary poet, just listen to the modest, self-knowing humanity in the opening lines of the poem where the "fragrant grasses" appear, as Li sits before a mirror, viewing herself with the clarity of an aging but unclouded eye, and reflects on this royal summons:

Untalented and sickly,
 I ring the dragon bell of age,
yet my hollow, undeserving name
 has reached the emperor.
Glancing up, I humbly place my ceremonial headpiece
 over my graying hair,
and with regret, wipe the mirror clear
 to fix my fading complexion.

What a tragic twist and loss, then, when Li, a poet who could write in her younger years about her Daoist contemplation with such unfeigned innocence in the poem below, was trapped by a historical entanglement that led to the same ruler ordering Li's execution just one year after she abandoned her hermit's naturalist practices and left her secluded residence to obey and serve at the behest of the emperor's summons.

My mind is a distant drifting cloud—
    I know it won't return.
It lives with clouds
    in the space
between existing and the Void.

Why do gusting winds
    scatter it about,
blowing back and forth
    from the southern
to the northern mountains?

While these poets certainly witnessed and participated in helping to create the golden poetic era of Chinese civilization, they and the populace at large also suffered from long periods of war and injustice. And, as female poets, they relentlessly struggled against the rigorous limitations of a male-dominated society for artistic, emotional, spiritual, and financial independence befitting their talent—not an easy undertaking for women of any class or caste at the time, and most especially for these poets. All of this is transmitted through their poetry, which we believe resonates in no small way with the lives of many women in today's contemporary world.

It must be said, however, because important details of the real experience of women's lives during this time period are barely known by anyone but scholars—and many myths obscure what really comprised their lives—that despite the aforementioned rigors, limitations, and subjugations, female poets and practitioners of the Dao were also able to enjoy certain benefits of a cosmopolitan empire during a period quite unique for many Chinese women. Particular classes of Tang women were free to divorce and remarry, for example, or even to take lovers. They had unprecedented access to education and were able to leave their marks as unique individuals in fields traditionally reserved for men, such as statesmanship, literature, and religious leadership.[1] (We encourage readers to turn to our afterword, The World of the Poets, found on p. 142 for a fascinating and more complete discussion of important historical aspects of the world and culture that so deeply influenced the lives and work of the poets.)

Yet even the relatively small class of women who benefited from these more positive circumstances still struggled with a society and culture that remained heavily controlled by men.[2] If all of this sounds familiar, it should. Similarities in women's lives between Tang China and the Western modern period make the poems in this collection fresh and relevant, despite their coming from another place and culture, and from a time approximately thirteen hundred years in the past.

We have grouped our three Daoist poets together in part

because traditional Chinese literary critics acknowledge the commonalities in the work and lives of Li Ye, Xue Tao, and Yu Xuanji. As noted, all three displayed striking poetic talent at an astonishingly young age. In addition, the naturalist and mystical Tang Daoism the poets found fundamental to their lives proves another salient organizing factor. Li Ye and Yu Xuanji were both Daoist priestesses, steeped in the traditions, myths, legends, and practices of the Dao, which, as we have noted, had strong ties to goddess culture at the time. In fact, the alchemical and erotic practices of Tang Daoism, whose existence is almost completely unknown in the contemporary Western world, allowed them a measure of physical, financial, and emotional independence that strongly influenced their writing. Xue Tao, on the other hand, was less fortunate because of her background as a courtesan, yet her dedication to Daoism as a householder practitioner has clear influence on her poems.

One other underlying factor of no small importance that brings these three poets together is the fierce independent voices that reverberate in their work. Whether expressing the depth of their spiritual practice, their feeling of connection to the natural world, or the often hard-wrought candid emotion that cuts to the core of what they felt needed to be said in direct, symbolic, or imagistic ways, these women express a kind of poetic charisma or charge—a refusal to hold back despite the social signals the culture sometimes used to keep such expression in check.

To illustrate the kind of candor that addresses the social circumstances and the feelings these conditions brought to the surface for these poets, here are lines by Yu Xuanji and Xue Tao.

Yu's poem expresses the bitterness of not being allowed to take the national exam because of her gender, when the subject was *poetry*, of all things. She knew, of course, that placing highly in that examination would not only grant her the official recognition for her poetic talent that she deserved but also allow her to advance her social and economic status, an advancement she sorely needed at the time. It is no wonder that her disappointment and bitterness was so profound. Yu writes these lines just after reading the posted list of male honorees. The image of "brutal hooks" in the first line of this excerpt refers both to the ideographs written by the selected male winners and the social constraints that held her back.

> Clear, brutal hooks form beneath their fingers!
> I hate that my poems must hide beneath my woman's robes—
> I lift my head in vain and envy the names of their honorees.

And here is Xue Tao, in quite a different mood from Yu, ending a most candid and tender poem written to her lover:

> Now that I'm old, not able to get things done,
> let me confess only to you—
> I wish I'd been able to have raised a son.

———

Poetry of any time period is best appreciated and enjoyed when it can be read without interruption. Books of poetry in translation often depend upon copious notes, usually placed in footnotes or at the back of the book, to help readers enter the world of the poetry at hand. It is a time-honored practice that often proves of use. While we have provided a scaled-down section of significant notes at the back of the book, including relevant myths and legends, to inform and encourage enjoyment of the poetry for readers, we decided not to follow this pattern entirely because many readers find it somewhat disruptive to the enjoyment found in reading poetry. Since this is the case, for any poem where we felt that a reader, *before* their first reading of the poem, would benefit from knowing the symbolic foundation or meaning of particular images, which might otherwise be obscured by culture or time, or any historical aspect significantly relevant to the poetry, we created a headnote written with pertinent information that we believe will be both informative and whetting of the reader's appetite to read on. We hope you find this approach appealing. And as you will see when you get to the individual poets themselves, we also have included a brief biography at the start of each poet's selections.

Finally, while our rigorous research into the language of the poems, and its particular usage during the period in which they were written, made it possible for us to remain faithful to the letter and spirit of the original ideographs that constitute these poems, we are aware that certain elements of bringing poetry forward from Tang Dynasty Chinese to contemporary North American English had to be navigated. For example, it is impossible for the English language to approximate the sound of the Chinese language in use now or at the time when these poems were written. The aural aspect of poetry is no small thing; the sound of words in a poem—the prosody, as it were—echoes and creates personal meaning and emotion for poet and reader alike. But with regard to these two languages, nothing can be done. In addition, since in our view it is important for translators to remain faithful to the original meaning and spirit of the poems at the time they were created, while maximizing the expression in English so that readers may have as full an experience of the poems as possible, there were times when we did not adhere to the usually accepted left-margin formatting many translators have used when bringing poems from classical Chinese literature into English. Instead, we relied on contemporary poetic phrasing, form, and line breaks to carry the full expression of the poems across.

While some may consider this a liberty, our decision to allow the form to be driven by the content allowed us to emphasize the phrasing, rhythm, and feeling found in the original poems in a way that might not otherwise be apparent or experienced by readers. This approach also brings out the vivid and uniquely symbolic imagery found in these remarkable poems in a manner that we feel best serves the enjoyment and understanding of English-language readers in the twenty-first century.

The act of translation, after all, is not solely a matter of transcribing the literal meaning of words on a page as it is brought from one language to another. Rather, it is about bringing the ineffable world of meaning, feeling, association, and imagination found in the original words to others in a faraway land and time with an intentional rigor that is authentic, faithful, and as complete as possible. In our approach, we tried to be sensitive, of course, to the needs of both the poems and readers while keeping in mind a sensibility expressed beautifully by the poet John Keats: "The reader completes the poem." It is our hope that in reading the work by these phenomenal poets, all readers may find such acts of completion, wherein the alchemy of poetry takes place, to be of the greatest satisfaction.

Peter Levitt   Rebecca Nie
Salt Spring Island, BC   Los Altos, CA

ACKNOWLEDGMENTS

The highly influential Japanese potter, writer, and philosopher Kawai Kanjiro (1890–1966 C.E.) wrote a book titled *We Do Not Work Alone*. This is certainly the case for artists of every kind. It is in this spirit that we offer our sincere gratitude and love to our spouses, Shirley Graham and Paul Simeon, for their unending support during the years we spent translating this work. To have the refuge of the homes and family life they make with us is a true treasure. We also thank Yuming Wang and Atman Partners, for their generous support that helped to make this book possible, and our agent, Anne Edelstein, for her kind contribution to the creation of *Yin Mountain*. And, finally, we offer our editors, Matt Zepelin and Emily Coughlin, our most joyous and heartfelt thanks for their belief in the importance of bringing the work of our three poets to readers in the twenty-first century and ensuring that the final book is of the highest quality in every regard.

LI YE

Li Ye (ca. 732–784 c.e.), also known as Li Jilan, was a poet and Daoist priestess from present-day Zhejiang Province. In *The Complete Collection of Tang Poems*, she is described as both talented and beautiful. When Li Ye was five years old, she made a spontaneous poem about roses for her father. It is said that the poem was so good that it made a lasting impression on her father and his guest. Afterward, her father made the remarkable statement, given the historical circumstance of their place and time, that for Li to marry would be a waste of her potential.

The next time Li Ye appears in the historical record she was a full-grown woman known as a Daoist priestess who was also famous for her calligraphy, poetry, and music. Since Tang Daoist priestesses were not bound by marital obligations, she had the full ability to freely associate with men. Li Ye enjoyed this freedom and became friends with many male intellectuals of the day, enjoying exchanges with cultural icons including Lu Yu, "the Sage of Tea," credited with creating the tea ceremony. She also had a love affair with the poet Yan Bojun (756–779 c.e.) and perhaps with some other poets.

Her life as a Daoist priestess and extraordinary poet led Li Ye's contemporary poet Liu Zhangqing to refer to her as a "poetic hero among women." Later literary critiques in *Background Matter of Tang Poems* described her poems as "masculine in form and essence while conceptually open and unrestrained."[3] Word of Li Ye's talent eventually reached the capital where in the spring of 783 c.e., Emperor Dezong summoned her to court to teach the royals. This was a great honor to bestow on any spiritual teacher.

Unfortunately, in the fall of that year, General Zhu Ci rebelled against the emperor and laid siege to the capital. Living in the emperor's palace, Li Ye feared for her life and went into hiding, but she was captured by the rebels and forced to write poems justifying Zhu Ci's military actions against the crown. In a terrible twist of fate and favor, after the rebellion was quashed the following year, these poems were used as evidence of Li Ye's coconspiracy with the general. The emperor ordered Li Ye to be executed in 784 c.e., despite the outcry by others in his court.

Centuries after Li Ye's demise, Chinese literary circles tightened the noose around her reputation when they became controlled by orthodox Confucian scholars who closely subscribed to the patriarchal ideal. Their agenda-driven interpretation of Li Ye's poetry depicted her as a perfect counter-ideal for how women ought to be in their male-dominated moral system. These scholars even used some of Li's innocent lines of spiritual content as evidence of her licentious, seductive nature.

Fortunately, recent academic research into Tang culture and related excavations present us with evidence to subvert these orthodox interpretations. We are grateful to be able to offer Li Ye's words as written to further open the door for contemporary readers to this remarkable Daoist poet-priestess.

神女天籟

Daoism and Goddess Culture

———

偶居

ACCIDENTAL ABIDING

While many contemporary people with a meditation practice may be able to relate to Li Ye's experience during her Daoist contemplation, especially the wayward nature of her mind as expressed in the second stanza of this poem, the space to which she refers in the first stanza is a recurring theme in Daoist philosophy. It is indicative of the Daoist view of the fluid nature of existence that flows as a manifestation of the nondual Void within the seemingly dualistic world of people, places, and things. To highlight how primary the Void is in Daoism, some texts refer to the Void as "the Mother of All Things."

My mind is a distant drifting cloud—
    I know it won't return.
It lives with clouds
    in the space
between existing and the Void.

Why do gusting winds
    scatter it about,
blowing back and forth
    from the southern
to the northern mountains?

心遠浮雲知不還，心雲并在有無間。
狂風何事相搖蕩，吹向南山復北山。

明月夜留別

DEPARTING ON A MOONLIT NIGHT

According to Chinese mythology, the Yellow Emperor, one of the legendary founders of China and Daoism, arrived at what is known as the Celestial Palace and learned the secret of immortality by seducing the Western Queen Mother, who lived in the palace with her entourage of goddesses.

As we depart,
  there is nothing to say
    beneath the silent moon,
      whose light
    reflects the way we truly feel.

From here on,
  we will long for each other
    like the moon
      floating between clouds,
    beyond the water,
  until it reaches
    the Celestial Palace.

離人無語月無聲，明月有光人有情
別後相思人似月，雲間水上到層城。

湖上卧病喜陸鴻漸至

SICK ON A LAKE AND HAPPILY RECEIVING LU HONGJIAN

Lu Hongjian, whose name appears in the title, was also famously known as Lu Yu, the author of *The Classic of Tea* in the late eighth century. Lu was revered as "the Sage of Tea" and credited with creating the tea ceremonies of China and Japan. Certainly Li Ye was aware of the Sage's drink of preference. Nonetheless, she invites her guest to share the elixir of Tao Yuanming, a seminal fourth-century hermit-poet known for his propensity for drinking, while they recite the poems of another hermit-poet, Xie Ke. Li's gesture to her guest is provocative to be sure.

Yesterday, you left beneath a moon thick with frost—
today you return to find me suffering beneath a bitter fog.
Still bedridden and ill,
only tears flow when I try to speak.
Let's just drink Tao's hermitage elixir,

and recite the poems of Xie Ke's seclusion.
Besides the slight chance we'll get drunk,
what else can we do?

昔去繁霜月，今來苦霧時。
相逢仍臥病，欲語淚先垂。
強勸陶家酒，還吟謝客詩。
偶然成一醉，此外更何之。

賦得三峽流泉歌

A SONG TO THE SPRING
OF THREE GORGES

The concept of one's original home, or source, is found in Daoism, Buddhism, and other major spiritual traditions. For a Daoist like Li Ye, it is the Dao itself, the way that cannot be expressed in words, even by a poet of her extraordinary talent, but is everywhere available. Li tells us that her original home can be found in the clouds that drift above Wu Mountain, where she and another of our poets, Xue Tao, find the Daoist goddess of erotic passion and intimate affairs. As noted in our preface, locating the Dao in a woman's sensuality, as Li and Xue do, is a powerful statement of Tang Daoist understanding that a woman's passion and physical, sensual nature is an embodiment of the Dao in female form. The fairly explicit sexual and erotic nature found in the rhythms and imagery of this poem are exemplary of the *yin* principle as Li intimately strums the song of her own woman's rapture on her "jade harp." They connect her with the powerful Mysterious Female that exists both in and beyond space and time as extolled in the Dao De Jing. Li expresses what may be considered the unity of the

Dao and her own woman's form in the melody where "cliffs and boulders collapse beneath my fingers" and "crashing waves come alive from the strings of my harp," just like in the age-old music she hears in her dreams.

My original home is in the clouds over Wu Mountain,
where I often hear the mountain's flowing spring waters—
a tune that rises out of my jade harp and orbits through space,
like the age-old music I hear in my dreams.
The Three Gorges that twist and turn for thousands of miles
drift into my secluded chamber in an instant—
cliffs and boulders collapse beneath my fingers,
rushing waterfalls and crashing waves come alive
from the strings of my harp.
Is it a raging wind, holding back thunder,
or the low moan of a river that cannot flow?
Soon, the strength of the roiling current will come to an end
and return to the peaceful trickle of water dripping on flat sand.
I recall the ancient times when Lord Ruan played this song,
and Zhong Rong just couldn't hear it enough.
After playing this piece one time, I will play it again—
may the music flow on, like a never-ending spring.

妾家本住巫山雲，巫山流泉常自聞。
玉琴奏出轉寥寞，直似當年夢裏聽。
三峽迢迢幾千里，一時流入幽閨裏。
巨石崩巖指下生，飛泉走浪絃中起。
初疑憤怒含雷風，又似嗚咽流不通。
回湍曲瀨勢將盡，時復滴瀝平沙中。
憶昔阮公為此曲，能令仲容聽不足。
一彈既罷還一彈，願似流泉鎮相續。

感興

FEELINGS ARISE

As many people will agree, the ineffable world of emotion is often given a voice through music. For some, the notes of a beautifully played composition comprise the only language that speaks what they feel. *Melody of Phoenix Pavilion*, which has such a strong effect on Li Ye in this poem, is a classic composition for Chinese harp, still widely performed today. It alludes both to a mythological tale and love stories known in China as far back as the seventh century B.C.E. As Li waits for her lover to return from his wandering, she finds herself thinking of the mythological male phoenix who flies all over the world in search of the perfect partner, resting only on the Chinese parasol tree and drinking from the purest springs. Li may well long for such a partner in early spring, marked by the return of the wild geese she sees in the sky. But in addition, one of the love stories the musical composition brings to mind is significant for her as a Daoist because it is one of the earliest mentions of a historical human becoming immortal through spiritual practice. It is also vital for the goddess culture and its traditions, so we will see references to it over and over in Li Ye's work.

From dawn to dusk, clouds and rain go hand in hand,
    the flight of wild geese
marks the time
    for my wandering man's return.

My jade pillow knows only
    the constant flow of tears,
the silver lamp shining
    in vain over my sleepless nights.

Lying face up, I watch as the bright moon
    tosses my hidden feelings around,
turning over, I see the running stream,
    and let my desire loose in a poem.

How I remember when I first heard
    Melody of Phoenix Pavilion—
now it just tumbles my loneliness
    into yearning once again.

朝雲暮雨鎮相隨，去雁來人有返期。
玉枕祇知長下淚，銀燈空照不眠時。
仰看明月翻含意，俯眄流波欲寄詞。
卻憶初聞鳳樓曲，教人寂寞復相思。

道意寄崔侍郎

DAOIST MESSAGE TO AN OFFICIAL

When Li Ye mentions the white hair forming at the temples of the official to whom she sends this poem, she is giving him a bit of a spiritual whack. While it may seem nothing more than a personal "dig" of sorts, she is relying on Daoist culture to point to the fact that in Chinese spiritual circles, a youthful look is typically considered a sign of spiritual attainment, and especially in Daoism where practices for men focus on longevity and immortality. But there is more. During the Tang period, Daoism and Buddhism were rivaling religions, and Buddhism, which came from India, was still considered somewhat foreign even during what may be thought of as its heyday in China. Since the history of Chinese culture includes a certain reluctance to accept other cultures and ways not of Chinese origin, perhaps this is the seed of both the chiding and Li's stern warning as the poem comes to an end.

> Quit your fascination with passing fame—
> think less about your position.
> Life passes swiftly like dawn to dusk,

your past striving comes to nothing at all.
The hair at your temples turns white from worry,
your long-life practices will fail.
Don't spend time on foreign teachings,
just follow the Daoist masters.

莫漫戀浮名，應須薄宦情。
百年齊旦暮，前事盡虛盈。
愁鬢行看白，童顏學未成。
無過天竺國，依止古先生。

柳

WILLOW

What I love most are the shallow banks
    where the river trickles around bends,
the sunset drifting shadows
    across petals of watercress.
Once again, the east wind washes
    everything with this year's green,
though the exiled hermit spreads her sorrow
    for thousands of miles in spring.

Low-hanging leaves conceal boats
    already straddling the shore,
the branches high up should cover
    those climbing the stairs.
Gradually, dancing figures move slowly
    as the smoky light grows old,
then fly off free as willow seeds
    to tease on the soft emerald bedding.

最愛纖纖曲水濱，夕陽移影過青蘋。
東風又染一年綠，楚客更傷千里春。
低葉已藏依岸棹，高枝應閉上樓人。
舞腰漸重煙光老，散作飛綿惹翠裀。

心聲情韻

Love Poems

———

相思怨

YEARNING LAMENT

Others say the ocean is deep,
　　but it's not half the depth of my yearning.
The sea is held in by the horizon,
　　but this longing goes on without end.
I carry my harp to the tower dome,
　　completely empty, filled with moonlight.
Strumming my desire into song,
　　my harp strings and heart come undone!

人道海水深，不抵相思半。
海水尚有涯，相思眇無畔。
攜琴上高樓，樓虛月華滿。
彈著相思曲，絃腸一時斷。

得閣伯鈞書

RECEIVING YAN BOJUN'S LETTER

Feelings rise as I face my mirror, too weary to comb my hair,
　　a cold evening rain batters the autumn trees in my yard.
Don't condemn the crisscrossing jade chopsticks,
　　threads of tears streaming down—
it's just my sorrow replying to the silver hooks of your writing.

情來對鏡懶梳頭，暮雨蕭蕭庭樹秋。
莫怪闌干垂玉箸，只緣惆悵對銀鈎。

寄朱放

TO ZHU FANG

Conservative Chinese historians have indicated a friendship be-
tween Li Ye and Zhu Fang, but the poetic evidence reveals that
their relationship was far more than that. A contemporary of Li
Ye's, Zhu Fang was a well-known hermit-poet with whom she
shared a feeling of great intimacy. Not only does Li Ye express the
extensive longing she feels during an interminable separation
from Zhu as she climbs into the mountains during yet another
springtime without him, but Zhu's poetry also expresses the heart-
break he felt when the two poets had to part. The restrained yet
charged emotional tone of this poem says it all.

Gazing at the water, I try to climb the mountain,
    its hills so high, the lake so wide.
With a longing that doesn't know dawn from dusk,
    my hope to see you has threaded months into years.
The tangled forest flourishes,
    wildflowers open softly across never-ending fields.
Our ceaseless feelings since parting
    will tumble out all at once when we finally meet.

望水試登山，山高湖又闊。
相思無曉夕，相望經年月。
鬱鬱山木榮，綿綿野花發。
別後無限情，相逢一時説。

送閻二十六赴剡縣

SENDING OFF YAN
TO SHAN COUNTY

While speaking with her lover, Yan, on the eve of his departure to the west, a journey that would take him far beyond the Gate of Paradise—a literal reference to the city of Suzhou, but also possibly an expression of Li's affection for him and all that they shared—Li weaves her sorrow together with a classical Chinese and Daoist legend. It was told that two young men, Liu Chen and Ruan Zhao, got lost while collecting medicinal herbs in Tiantai Mountain, a practice quite familiar to Daoists of that time. After wandering lost for thirteen days without food, they found a peach tree, ate some peaches, and then found a cup of rice floating down a stream. They ate the rice and followed the stream until they came upon the residence of two beautiful women who recognized them. The women received them with heavenly music, and during their time together they served the two lucky men opulent feasts. The young men stayed on as the women's consorts for about half a year before deciding to return home. After coming back, however, they realized that the women they had been with were goddesses and that ten generations had passed in the human realm. Liu then resumed his worldly life, married, and had children. Ruan had other aspirations and decided to return to the mountain to study the Dao.

The waterway flows out beyond the Gate of Paradise,
your lone boat will travel farther westward day after day.
The sorrow of parting pervades the fragrant grasses—
everywhere the desolation is lush.
My modest dreams weave through Wu Garden,
while your journey takes you to the River Shan.
If you return, please come to see me again—
don't get lost like youthful Ruan.

流水閶門外，孤舟日復西。
離情遍芳草，無處不淒淒。
妾夢經吳苑，君行到剡溪。
歸來重相訪，莫學阮郎迷。

八至

EIGHT EXTREMES

Nearest or farthest are East and West.
Deepest or shallowest is a clear stream.
Highest and brightest are the sun and the moon.
Most intimate or distant is a couple in bed.

至近至遠東西，至深至淺清溪。
至高至明日月，至親至疏夫妻。

春閨怨

BOUDOIR LAMENT IN SPRING

The innocent spring buds on the branching peach tree that appear here are well-known symbols of youth, liveliness, and longevity in Chinese culture, and especially in Daoist culture; they also represent female desire. Li does not shy away from the sensuality of the image, and especially in the larger context of this poem where the symbolism in the original alludes to a third-century B.C.E. prose text written by Song Yu, where a beautiful woman covets and even chases after her man. We've taken the liberty of deconstructing the symbolic imagery found in the fourth line, which would be explicit for Chinese readers, in order to make its meaning more accessible in English. It is notable in this poem and others how freely Li expresses female desire, despite living in the male-dominated Tang period. This short poem certainly ends with a surprising twist.

Above the railing of a hundred-foot well,
peach branches have already budded red.
Thinking of you, far off by the harsh northern sea,
tosses me in the direction of intriguing men.

百尺井闌上，數枝桃已紅。
念君遼海北，拋妾宋家東。

薔薇花

ROSES

Once again, Li feels completely free to allow the poem's imagery
to express her own sensuality as she gazes at an array of beautiful
and innocent roses and finds their sensuality as well. Readers
might even momentarily forget the apparent subject of the poem
and think that it speaks symbolically only of the allure and passion
of young women. With the support of female Daoist and goddess
culture practices, Li's voice is suitably empowered to make the
connections she does.

Jade-green and scarlet blossoms blend together effortlessly—
leaning against the railing like show-offs,
the fragrance from their deep place seduces butterflies
who fear picking their flaming petals that burn in spring.
Hanging in midair—they weave a delicate canopy,
touching ground—they reveal a gorgeous embroidered lingerie.
Best seen in the wee hours, still wet with dew—
a fresh stem outside the green silk screen.

翠融紅綻渾無力，斜倚欄干似詫人。
深處最宜香惹蝶，摘時兼恐焰燒春。
當空巧結玲瓏帳，著地能鋪錦繡裀。
最好凌晨和露看，碧紗窗外一枝新。

詩書往來

Poems in Correspondence

———

結素魚貽友人

TYING WHITE SILK FISH
TO GIVE TO A FRIEND

People in the Tang period sent letters to each other enclosed in
various items marked with fish designs that served as envelopes.
Li refers to that practice here.

I take a few feet of snow-white silk
and knot it into a pair of carp.
If you want to know what's in my heart,
just take a look at the words in their bellies.

數尺如殘雪，結為雙鯉魚。
欲知心裏事，看取腹中書。

送韓揆之江西

SEEING OFF HAN KUI TO JIANGXI

We'd like to offer a linguistic insight into the subtlety of the first image in the poem: willow branches. In Chinese, the pronunciation of the character 柳, "weeping willow," is so close to the inflected pronunciation for 留, which means "stay," that Tang people often presented a gift of willow branches to parting friends or family when saying farewell. It is this kind of quiet, nuanced use of language, often merging images from the natural world with emotion, that contributed to admiration for Li Ye's poetry. The depth of Li's feeling here is emphasized by the final natural image, which makes clear that this parting will be of quite a long duration, and possibly one without end.

> We look at each other while breaking off willow branches,
> our sorrowful parting entwined with these tender vines
>   that stir in the wind.
>
> In the ten thousand miles of Jiangxi's waters,
> to what place can your lone boat return?

The tides don't travel as far as Pen City,
and word is rarely received in Xiakou.

Only wild geese from the deep south
fly back and forth year after year.

相看折楊柳，別恨轉依依。
萬里江西水，孤舟何處歸。
溢城潮不到，夏口信應稀。
唯有衡陽雁，年年來去飛。

寄校書七兄

POEM TO PROOFREADER ELDER BROTHER SEVEN

In this affectionate poem, the Daoist poet Li Ye uses the term "elder brother" to remind her friend of their close relationship while also offering her understanding that mortals live between the world of earth and the heavens, where Trembling Star (Venus, in the west) keeps a watchful eye, and more far off, there is the world of the Immortals. Readers will find an echo here of her poem "Accidental Abiding" (page 7), where she says that her mind "lives with clouds / in the space / between existing and the Void." What greater treasure, then, could she seek than to have her elder brother reply with a poem?

> There's nothing to do in Wucheng County
> but watch the months, years, and more pass by—
> not knowing how my minister in Yun Pavilion is doing,
> how lonesome you must feel.
> An Immortal's boat drifts on distant waters,

while Trembling Star accompanies your stately coach.
As you travel past the shores of Great Thunder,
don't forget to reply with an eight-line poem.

無事烏程縣，蹉跎歲月餘。
不知芸閣吏，寂寞竟何如。
遠水浮仙棹，寒星伴使車。
因過大雷岸，莫忘八行書。

思命追入留別廣陵故人

AFTER RECEIVING THE IMPERIAL SUMMONS, FAREWELL TO MY OLD FRIENDS IN GUANGLIN

Writing in her later years, Li Ye startles with this opening image and then fills the poem with symbolic allusion. For the poet's name to reach the emperor is no small accomplishment, since the characters she chooses for "emperor" also refer to the heavenly imperial court in the Daoist pantheon. It appears that in preparation for her journey to the palace, Li tries on a ceremonial headpiece as she sits before her mirror. In the Tang Dynasty, the headpieces of Daoist priestesses were so elaborate that they influenced the Tang fashion scene as well. Historically, Li seems to have been summoned to teach the "fragrant grasses" in the palace harem, and so she must leave her residence, where she engages in her naturalist hermit practices as a "wild guest," to follow the pathway of sand gulls in their freeing flight. It is interesting to note that sand gulls and many other white seabirds are symbols of Daoist practitioners with esteemed reputations. Legend says that Immortals live on

selected mountainous islands in the Pacific Ocean, where all the
animals and birds are white.

> Untalented and sickly,
>> I ring the dragon bell of age,
> yet my hollow, undeserving name
>> has reached the emperor.
> Glancing up, I humbly place my ceremonial headpiece
>> over my graying hair,
> and with regret, wipe the mirror clear
>> to fix my fading complexion.
> Here, my mind darts through the northern palace gate,
>> following the fragrant grasses,
> eyes scanning the southern mountains
>> to gaze at the ancient peaks.
> The cinnamon trees
>> cannot keep this wild guest from leaving—
> sand gulls take off freely from their shallow banks
>> to meet in the sky.

無才多病分龍鍾，不料虛名達九重。
仰愧彈冠上華髮，多慙拂鏡理衰容。
馳心北闕隨芳草，極目南山望舊峯。
桂樹不能留野客，沙鷗出浦漫相逢。

XUE TAO

———

薛濤

Xue Tao was arguably one of the most celebrated female poets of the Tang dynastic period. Operas were written about her, and public monuments were erected in her name. Even to this day in Chengdu, the well from which Xue Tao drew water is a well-known attraction for visitors and tourists alike. One reason Xue Tao received so much attention was that her talent and life exemplified the courtesan-poet archetype that fascinated and entertained the imaginations of men who maintained the Confucian orientation during and after her life. Unfortunately, many of these scholars also created fantasies and composed stories about Xue Tao that proved confusing to a clear understanding of her life's actual events.

Even the dates of Xue Tao's life are a matter of academic debate. By analyzing multiple period-appropriate sources, the scholar Chen Wenhua demonstrated that Xue Tao most likely lived between 758 C.E. and 832 C.E. We know without question, however, that Xue Tao was wellborn and that her family name suggests a connection with the high-level aristocracy of her day. Her father, Xue Yun, moved for government work from their clan's home base in the capital to Chengdu in southwestern China when Xue Tao was quite young. By the tender age of eight, Xue Tao's talent in music and poetry was already being nourished by a quality education.

One day, it is told, as Xue Tao and her father sat in the family courtyard, her father pointed to the parasol tree near their water well and started a poem:

> An ancient parasol in our courtyard—
> its upright trunk punctures the clouds.

And without a moment's hesitation, young Xue Tao completed the poem:

> Her branches welcome birds from the North and South,
> her leaves mingle back and forth with the wind.

The exchange made her father anxious for quite some time. Was it her awareness of the receptivity associated with *yin* at such a young age? Unfortunately, Xue Yun passed away when Xue Tao was still a child, and Xue Tao was partly raised by her widowed mother to be a young woman known for her beauty and poetic talent. Mysteriously, as youth turned to young womanhood, she also became a courtesan.

It is not clear how this wellborn girl came to enter the courtesan caste, especially since women and men of the entertainment and courtesan caste were highly marginalized by Tang laws and institutions that prohibited those in the caste from participating in professions other than entertainment and sex work. They were also forbidden to marry outside of their caste or to ordain as members of religious institutions. Many such women started out life as homeless children and, in the end, were trafficked as sex workers. Some commoner women fell into the entertainment and courtesan caste because of financial destitution, but there is no solid historical evidence that this was Xue Tao's circumstance. It is not surprising that Tang courtesan women faced severe abuses, and most fared poorly. However, some courtesans were able to achieve financial success and fame, and Xue Tao was undoubtedly one of those who did.

Throughout her career, Xue Tao entertained wealthy and influential patrons. At the age of twenty-seven, she was discovered by Wei Gao, the military governor of Xichuan Circuit, who made her his official hostess. Wu Yuanheng, one of the subsequent military governors, even wrote to the emperor requesting permission to formally employ Xue Tao as a secretary, and Xue Tao's biography in *The Complete Library of Four Collections* records many banquet exchanges Xue Tao had with Wu and other high-aristocratic men. In fact, a great number of Xue Tao's surviving poems are composed in correspondence with them.

As expected from women in her position, Xue Tao also engaged in romantic relationships with several well-to-do members of the ruling class. The most well-known affair involving Xue was with Yuan Zhen, a seminal Tang literary figure who later became the empire's prime minister. We have included poems that stem from this romance so that readers can appreciate Xue's feelings with regard to her relationship with Yuan Zhen.

In her old age, Xue Tao retired to her country home by Flower Rinsing Creek and dedicated herself to art and the further development of her spiritual life. She wore Daoist vestments and continued to compose poems and make an artisanal paper that is still celebrated today. Xue Tao passed away when she was almost eighty years old, leaving behind more than five hundred poems.

神女天籟

Daoism and Goddess Culture

送扶鍊師

TO ALCHEMIST FU

In Xue Tao's poems, the clouds above Wu Gorge are not simply a matter of weather. They refer to the Daoist goddess of erotic passion and affairs, Princess Yao. Always a free-spirited and passionate girl, legend tells us that the goddess accidentally died young near the Wu Gorge. From then on, practitioners believed that she took the form of the gorge's clouds and, at will, transformed into a beautiful maiden so she might entice and make love with male travelers who suited her fancy. Possibly these affairs were located on the *yin* slope, since in the Chinese worldview, *yin* is regarded as the "female principle." Manifesting the qualities of shadow, darkness, and mystery, *yin* also represents anything internal or still, in addition to moisture, water, and earth. Rain is a frequent imagistic reference to *yin*, and the phrase "clouds and rain" often refers to lovemaking. Perhaps, taken as a whole, this is why *yin* also represents fertility and reproduction, and is an adjective for female internal organs and receptivity.

Beneath clouds gathering above Wu Gorge
    the boat returns to the burnished shore,
the distant green waves
    pounded by heavy rains.

The wondrous practices on the mountain's *yin* slope
    have been talked about for many years,
like the gifts of geese
    to calligraphy master Youjun.

錦浦歸舟巫峽雲，綠波迢遞雨紛紛。
山陰妙術人傳久，也説將鵝與右軍。

聽僧吹蘆管

LISTENING TO A BUDDHIST MONK PLAY REED FLUTE

The soft cry of morning cicadas,
    the sorrow of evening warblers,
flow from your fingertips
    like gentle speech.

You set aside reading scriptures
    to trouble yourself with a tune—
improvising to the sound of temple chimes,
    it's just like the purity of autumn.

曉蟬嗚咽暮鶯愁，言語殷勤十指頭。
罷閱梵書勞一弄，散隨金磬泥清秋。

酬楊供奉法師見招

RESPONSE TO YANG GONGFENG FASHI'S SUMMONS

Myths and stories about hermits who lived in the mountains in ancient China have captured the contemporary imagination. Many of us have the impulse to leave our crazy-busy lives behind, thinking that a hermit's life would be far preferable, though the reality of such a life might give us a different point of view. By the end of the Qin Dynasty (ca. 200 B.C.E.), there were four hermits living on Shang Mountain. Their fame spread far and wide, and they were admired by many good people for maintaining their way of life.

About four hundred years later, at the end of the Han Dynasty (ca. 200 C.E.), a hermit named Yuan An lived in Luo Yang. One night, a fierce and all-encompassing snowstorm struck Luo Yang, driving many common people into destitution. It is said that Yuan An faced and braved the storm by staying in his humble hut, thereby keeping to his hermit ways rather than flee. As a result, he froze and starved. When the strength of his determination and way became known, the local magistrate recommended Yuan An to join the court. It makes us smile to imagine his response when he received the invitation.

> Like a secluded river
>> that flows purely without ceasing,
> you recline behind snow-packed windows,
>> level with the clouds.
> Not belittling Yuan's hut,
>> with neither fire nor smoke,
> you can only smile at the fame
>> such hermits have brought to Shang Mountain.

遠水長流潔復清，雪牕高臥與雲平。
不嫌袁室無煙火，惟笑商山有姓名。

石斛山曉望寄呂侍御

MORNING POEM FROM ORCHID MOUNTAIN TO LYU SHIYU

Xue Tao's familiarity and comfort with Chinese mythology, especially when it comes to elements of the natural world, weave together in many poems with her more personal intimate relationships. Using the name Mysterious Sunshine in reference to her friend Lyu Shiyu—in a poem that also acknowledges the great Mother Sun Goddess, who brings light and life to each day—may very well be part of the poet's overall vision that sees heaven and earth, humans, Immortals, and goddesses as belonging to one another.

Mother Sun Goddess spins her wheel,
    casting first light against the Immortals' windows.
Morning's mountain wind
    spirals mist deeply into the boundless sky.
Mysterious Sunshine, you're not here with me,
    but we can still point with awe
to dark forests in distant corners of the world,
    brushed with emerald green.

曦輪初轉照仙扃，旋擘煙嵐上窅冥。
不得玄暉同指點，天涯蒼翠漫青青。

謁巫山廟

PILGRIMAGE TO THE TEMPLE
OF WU MOUNTAIN

The pilgrimage Xue Tao makes in this poem is largely one of the imagination as she enters the realm of legend from the time of Chu culture, which dates as far back as 1000 B.C.E. During that period, both shamanism and proto-Daoism were supported. In addition to this disposition toward spiritual expression, the time of Chu showed a leaning toward the simple seeking of pleasure, which some conservative Chinese historians have considered decadent behavior.

Gaotang was the name of a Daoist temple on Wu Mountain, and it was here, legend tells us, that the Goddess of Wu Mountain may have engaged in one of her mythological lovemaking rituals with none other than the ancestral king of Chu, a forefather of King Qing. Not one to keep a secret, this affair was recorded forever by the poet and diviner Song Yu, whose good looks were also a matter of legend. As Xue Tao allows her imagination to lead her past the howling apes in her journey to the ruins of the sanctuary itself, she discovers the echoes of these tales embedded in the natural setting that remains, and experiences a melancholy feeling, since the time of Chu's sexually charged "clouds and rain" had long before come to an end.

Seeking Gaotang Sanctuary amid the bedlam of howling apes,
I follow a path through the iridescent mist of twilight clouds,
the scent of woodland grass and trees.

The mountain colors have not forgotten Song Yu,
the rivers still weep and mourn for King Qing.
So many days and nights were spent beneath that Sun's tower,
until Chu's clouds and rain finally came to an end.

I hardly know how many willows face this melancholy shrine,
but the spacious quiet of this hollow-feeling spring
struggles with the trilling laughter of a thrush.

亂猿啼處訪高唐，　路入煙霞草木香。
山色未能忘宋玉，　水聲猶是哭襄王。
朝朝夜夜陽臺下，　為雨為雲楚國亡。
惆悵廟前多少柳，　春來空門畫眉長。

試新服裁製初成三首

THREE POEMS FOR TRYING
NEW DAOIST GARMENTS

One

If there is *yin*, there is *yang*; if there is *yang*, there is *yin*. These
two words refer to the Daoist understanding of the seemingly
dualistic forces that unify and thereby lie at the root of all things.
It is by working together in a way that is complementary and
interconnected that the active principle of *yang* and the recep-
tive principle of *yin* help the world to come into existence in a
balanced way. Since purple is the color of *yang*, naming it along-
side *yang*, as Xue Tao does in the first line, indicates the highest
expression of the *yang* principle, and so it might be noted that
according to legend, it is in the Purple Yang Palace that the Dao-
ist Immortals reside.

In the first of these three poems, we meet Chang-eh, the
Moon Goddess. At one time alive in human form, Chang-eh con-
sumed an elixir of immortality of such great potency that it lifted
her out of the human realm until she found herself living for

eternity in the cold and barren Moon Palace with her white rabbit as her only companion.

In an act of compassionate affection, the poet causes Chang-eh, possibly in remembrance of her own warmer days, to point to Weaver Star's Bridge in the Milky Way so that the lovers Weaving Girl (the star Vega) and Cowherd (the star Altair) may rush across it to be together, which Chinese legend says they do once a year on the seventh day of the seventh month. In this way, Xue Tao may imply the *yin* and *yang* principles are also the source of love.

> The Purple Yang Palace endows me with this raw red silk,
> translucent as the immortal mists far off at sea.
> Cold as a frost rabbit's fur, still as an icy cocoon,
> Chang-eh points to Weaver Star's Bridge with a smile.

紫陽宮裏賜紅綃，仙霧朦朧隔海遙。
霜兔毿寒冰繭靜，嫦娥笑指織星橋。

Two

The word *qi* (sometimes written as *chi*) refers to the primordial essence of things, a fundamental concept in Daoism. When referring to a person's qi, it means "pneuma," "the breath," "the vital spirit or soul" that animates a human being. When it refers to inanimate objects or places, it refers loosely to what might be understood as an aura. In Western parlance, qi is used to mean "energy." In the first line of this poem, Xue refers to the "nine primordial essences." These are the universal essences that connect the heavenly bodies (expressed as the stars in the Big Dipper) with the major organs in the human body. Each of the essences also has a color associated with it, which Xue was clearly aware of when composing the first line. As part of erotic Daoist rituals, some Tang and pre-Tang Daoist texts provocatively state that during foreplay, fully aroused women spontaneously express the qi of these primordial essences stored in their bodies and thereby channel the celestial essences while making love. The "five immortal spirits" that appear in the second line of the poem are the unicorn, the phoenix, the turtle, the dragon, and the white tiger. They are also auspicious signs of kings. And the Eastern Lord is, of course, the sun, though it also refers to the god of spring.

> The nine primordial essences
> > thread into luminous shades of dawn,
> as five immortal spirits
> > steer their five-cloud carriage.
> When the spring winds weave
> > through the Eastern Lord's Palace,
> they snatch the hundred-flower quilt
> > that colors the world.

九氣分為九色霞，　五靈仙馭五雲車。
春風因過東君舍，　偷樣人間染百花。

Three

Daoist lore reveals an extensive, subtle, and sophisticated spiritual expression, exemplified by the use of symbolic naming. It was commonly understood that the Daoist Immortals have many abodes, often carrying a name that evoked a spiritual attribute valued in Daoism. In the first of these three poems, they reside in the Purple Yang Palace; in this poem they make their home with the gods on a level of Daoist heaven known as Supreme Clarity, which is also the name of an early Daoist denomination. The rite where practitioners hoped to engage with the Immortals included the use of the cloud-shaped jade Ganoderma mushroom, which legend said could be transformed into an elixir of immortality. We can only imagine the singing, dancing, and chants that took place in these group rituals that included the provocatively named ode "Steps of the Void."

> Originally, this long skirt
>   was for the rite of Supreme Clarity,
> where people grasped sacred mushrooms
>   and pursued gatherings of Immortals.
> During every temple get-together
>   for song and dance,
> they bowed and chanted
>   the ode "Steps of the Void."

長裙本是上清儀，曾逐羣仙把玉芝。
每到宮中歌舞會，折腰齊唱步虛詞。

賦凌雲寺

ODE TO BEYOND CLOUD TEMPLE

Reference to the Western Queen Mother in Chinese mythology can be found in oracle bone carvings that date back to around the fifteenth century B.C.E. As Daoism developed, she was understood to be the goddess of life and immortality. Xue Tao brings this aspect of the goddess into the poem with her reference to the Jade Platform, a monument for ceremonies and gatherings of the Immortals found in the Celestial Palace of the Western Queen Mother.

I have heard about blossoms
    at Beyond Cloud Temple
that leap into the air,
    swirl past the stone steps,
and chase along the river bends!

But now and then they cling
    to Chang-eh's moon mirror
and engrave the iridescent Jade Platform
    in the setting sun.

聞説凌雲寺裏花，飛空遶磴逐江斜。
有時鑷得嫦娥鏡，鏤出瑤臺五色霞。

九日遇雨

NINTH DAY, CAUGHT IN THE RAIN

The festival in this poem refers to the annual Double Yang Festival, celebrated on the ninth day of the ninth month. In Daoism, the number nine represents the active *yang* principle, and so Double Yang is considered a highly auspicious day. Lots of energy! Dating back almost two thousand years from contemporary times, the celebration always included the appearance of chrysanthemums, the drinking of chrysanthemum tea, offerings to ancestors made of the spiritual qualities found in certain foods, and hikes in the mountain air with family and friends. At the local festivals themselves, ornaments of golden glory branches and berries were often worn. With so much *yang* energy, it is no wonder that the goddess appears, with the sexual energy symbolized by clouds and rain covering the land below.

Golden glory ornaments—
    but the autumn festival
        has been held up!
Saffron chrysanthemums
    and fragrant chilly flowers
        fill the courtyard.
Knowing desire,
    the goddess
        is on her way down—
clouds and rain
    darkly
        cover the pond.

茱萸秋節佳期阻，金菊寒花滿院香。
神女欲來知有意，先令雲雨暗池塘。

海棠溪

APPLE CREEK

Spring guides this creek to its place in the immortal twilight,
    her waters and fish always bearing flowers.
But the human world doesn't cherish the blossoms as sacred,
    people just rush to dye their skimpy silks bright red.

春教風景駐仙霞，水面魚身總帶花。
人世不思靈卉異，競將紅纈染輕紗。

心聲情韻

Love Poems

———

鷹離鞲

HAWK SOARING AWAY

One of Xue Tao's *Ten Parting Poems*, "Hawk Soaring Away" has been celebrated as among her most penetrating expressions for more than one thousand years. Highly personal as well as culturally indicative, there is much to be found in these four short lines. The poet fell in love with the literary giant and successful minister Yuan Zhen. However, after what must have been an exceptionally contentious quarrel, she fell out of favor with this powerful man, who then refused to have contact with her. Over time she wrote ten poems comparing herself to rare animals or collectible objects to express her feelings, including regret. After reading the extraordinarily expressive work, Yuan Zhen changed his mind and the relationship temporarily resumed.

Read with contemporary eyes, this and other poems in the *Ten Parting Poems*, and the objectification displayed within them, are met with a great deal of dismay. The fact that any woman, much less a woman as aware, talented, and recognized as Xue Tao, would willingly compare herself to pets and collectibles

reveals the widespread acceptance of misogyny in Chinese cul-
ture. Even a woman with profound Daoist understanding was
not necessarily free of the trap. After all, the price paid by a
woman of excellent talent and soaring, independent imagina-
tion could be quite high, as revealed in the punishing final lines.
Though given the subtlety of her poetry, there is also the possibility
that Xue Tao intended them as a critique of the cultural restrictions
women endured.

With my talon spears and bell-like eyes,
my capturing of hares is praised by all,
but since I soared above the blue clouds for no reason,
you no longer let me perch on your arm.

爪利如鋒眼似鈴，平原捉兔稱高情。
無端竄向青雲外，不得而今手上擎。

雜詠：罰赴邊上武相公

TRIBUTE FOR WU XIANGGONG
GOING TO THE FRONT LINES

Wu Xianggong was a relative of the famous Empress Wu and an important patron of Xue Tao's; his support of her poetry lifted her out of obscurity. It is somewhat remarkable and bold that in the poem's title, Xue refers to him as Xianggong, since that is a term that wives typically used to refer only to their husbands. The images in the poem comprise an intimate and even somewhat flirtatious expression of her feelings. Since the poem was part of a popular game that combined drinking and poetry, where the loser needed either to drink more or compose a poem, it may have been written at a going-away banquet for Wu.

> Firefly in the barren wilds,
>> moon in the sky,
> how can she fly to the side
>> of the wheeling moon?

Their radiant light should shine for each other
    across ten thousand miles,
but clouds in the distant sky block her vision—
    her words can't make their way across.

螢在荒蕪月在天，螢飛豈到月輪邊。
重光萬里應相照，目斷雲霄信不傳。

江邊

THE RIVERBANK

As noted with regard to Li Ye's poem on page 39, "Tying White Silk Fish to Give to a Friend," in the Tang period, people sent letters to each other in various enclosures that served as envelopes. Often these cases displayed fish designs. How subtly Xue Tao points to the value of human relationships and communication, and how important these are for helping self and other to remain clear in a world where one can so easily be lost in a dream.

As the west wind brings pairs of swallows out of the blue,
both the human world and my heart naturally surrender.
If not for the true chanting hidden within fish,
who could stand in the clear river dream after dream?

西風忽報燕雙雙，人世心形兩自降。
不為魚腸有真訣，誰能梦梦立清江。

秋泉

A NATURAL SPRING IN AUTUMN

Frosted and starting to clear, just a ribbon of mist—
in the distance, a tune flows out of seclusion on ten silk strings.
Its lingering rhythm reaches my pillow to stir my longing
and keep this troubled woman from her midnight sleep.

冷色初澄一帶烟，幽聲遙瀉十絲絃。
長來枕上牽情思，不使愁人半夜眠。

望春詩

A POEM LOOKING
TOWARD SPRING

When flowers blossom, our joy is different,
when they fall, our sorrow is not the same.
If you want to ask about our yearning,
flowers bloom, and in time they fade.

花開不同賞，花落不同悲。
欲問相思處，花開花落時。

寄舊詩與微之

SENDING AN OLD-STYLE POEM
TO WEIZHI

The red paper Xue Tao mentions in this tender poem to her lover, Weizhi, a courtesy name for Yuan Zhen, was artisanal paper that the poet crafted herself. She would write poems on this paper and give them as gifts. The quality and style of the paper was so unique that it became the official court stationery and is still known in China to this day as "Xue Tao note paper." Given the passionate association of the color and the heartfelt confession in the poem, it seems likely this poem was written on such paper and offered to her lover as a most intimate gift.

Everyone knows your writing, music, and way,
but only I know the fine wind and light of your being.
While describing flowers on a moonlit night,
we were tender in the peaceful dark.
On rainy mornings we chanted beside each other
about willows that leaned so close.
For so long, I was taught to hide myself
like precious emerald jade,

but I always wrote on red paper
that you'd carry by your side.
Now that I'm old, not able to get things done,
let me confess only to you—
I wish I'd been able to have raised a son.

詩篇調態人皆有，細膩風光我獨知。
月夜詠花憐暗澹，雨朝題柳為欹垂。
長教碧玉藏深處，總向紅箋寫自隨。
老大不能收拾得，與君閒似教男兒。

詩書往來

Poems in Correspondence

送友人

TO A FRIEND

Night frost settles on the wetland reeds,
 the cold moon and mountain sharing indigo blue.
Who says thousands of miles between us begins tonight?
 Our dreams are as traceless as the Great Wall is long.

  水國蒹葭夜有霜，月寒山色共蒼蒼。
  誰言千里自今夕，離夢杳如關塞長。

送鄭眉州

TO ZHENG MEI ZHOU

Though Luo Fu, who figures in this poem, was a commoner in the second century C.E., some of her poetry was known. She came to symbolize intelligence, beauty, and faithfulness. As we have noted, in Daoism the *yin* principle is associated with the feminine characteristics of moisture, fluidity, and darkness, or what might be thought of as "the internal." Xue Tao shows Luo Fu, very much within herself, gazing from this vantage point at the distant soldiers below.

Rain darkens Eyebrow Mountain
    where torrential rivers flow.
Standing at a distance,
    a woman on a high tower hides behind her sleeves.
With double banners, thousands of riders
    gallop in formation along the eastern road.
Only the immaculate beauty, Luo Fu,
    gazes at them from above.

雨暗眉山江水流，離人掩袂立高樓。
雙旌千騎駢東陌，獨有羅敷望上頭。

別李郎中

FAREWELL TO LI LANGZHONG

In this poem for the poet Li Langzhong, Xue Tao relies on her considerable knowledge of Chinese literary history to help convey the depth of her distress at being parted from her lover. Anren, whose name appears in line five, is the courtesy name of the third-century C.E. poet Pan Yue, known for his handsome bearing and keen mind. Unfortunately, Pan Yue's personal history also included great tragedy. His wife died when they were young, which led him to write some of his most famous lines, which Xue Tao relies upon for the conceit of her poem:

> We were a pair of birds nesting in the woods.
> One woke in the morning to find himself alone.

Pan's fate was not limited to this loss, however. In the year 300 C.E., he was accused of plotting against the throne and he and his entire family were arrested and executed for the alleged crime. Indeed, as Xue Tao says, had he more time to write his poetry, much of it likely would be expressive exactly as Xue Tao describes.

When flowers drop from the parasol tree,
　　the phoenix leaves his mate behind.
Imagining you at the peak of the Sichuan Alps
　　is more miserable still.
Even if Anren had more that he could write,
　　half of his elegies would weave together
wretchedness and death.

花落梧桐鳳別凰，想登秦嶺更凄涼。
安仁縱有詩將賦，一半音詞雜悼亡。

YU XUANJI

魚玄機

Yu Xuanji was born in Chang'an, the Tang capital city, around the year 843 C.E., and executed there in 868 C.E., at the approximate age of only twenty-five. During her short life, she traveled the realm, navigated the landscape of complex and often treacherous social and religious strata, and inspired generations with her life, talent, and beauty.

Yu was born to commoner parents. Like other households in Chang'an, it is probable that her family rented a part of their residence to male scholars who participated in the national exam system, which provided the ability for those who did well to socially and financially advance to the ruling bureaucracy. The budding poetic prodigy likely received her literary education and met her future husband through her family's tenants. Tang culture took physical beauty as a sign of spiritual attainment and a claim of transcendence. As we will see in some poems from later in her life, Yu Xuanji leveraged this sentiment, in addition to her poetic talent, as she navigated the male-dominated social strata. Yu also showed a keen interest in Daoist spirituality at this early age, yet she went on to marry Li Zi'an when she was fifteen.

Throughout the Tang Dynasty, marriages were arranged between families of equal social status, while high-aristocratic families preferred to marry their daughters to young men who scored well in the national exams. Since Li Zi'an ranked first among the entire empire's scholars in his examination class, in marrying him, Yu had to be content with the status of Li's "second wife" or "lesser wife," which meant she was relegated to the position of a concubine despite the intimacy of their personal relationship and her exceptional poetic talent. This accorded with the custom of the time for well-to-do men to have one primary wife and many concubines, as well as the socially accepted ability of that class of men to have multiple love affairs with their maids and professional courtesans. The marital situation for women in this circumstance was, to say the least, difficult by any description. Primary wives were often wellborn yet received little affection in their politically motivated arranged marriages, while lesser wives were often subjected to horrific yet lawful physical abuse, ranging from frequent beatings to mutilation, disfigurement, and even death at the hands of the primary wives and their husbands.

As expressed in her poems, Yu was a favorite of Li Zi'an's during the early days of their relationship. He brought her with him when he took local positions in the provinces that advanced his situation, following a well-trodden early career path for Tang ministers. During these few years, Li sponsored Yu Xuanji's traveling, brought her with him to meet with friends, and even appeared with her publicly during a polo match. Unfortunately, the happy early days of their marriage did not last long, starting with Li Zi'an and Yu Xuanji moving back to Chang'an when he took a position at the central court. Despite the fact that both Yu's family and the family of Li Zi'an's highborn primary wife were from the capital, their respective class positions prevented any chance of common ground, and the apparent intimacy between Li Zi'an and Yu Xuanji inflamed envy and wrath from his primary wife. Shortly after their return to Chang'an, likely as a matter of forced separation, Yu Xuanji ordained as a Daoist priestess at Xianyi Convent when she was seventeen years old.

Xianyi Convent was an aristocratic establishment built for an imperial princess. Female members of official families were ordained and lived there while assuming public roles, as was also customary for Tang Daoist priestesses. Yu Xuanji enjoyed her freedom as a Daoist priestess, while her poetic talent and stunning appearance led her to quickly become a sensation among literary aristocrats in Chang'an. Her contemporaries wrote that Yu's "verses were often widely circulated among a forest of aristocrats" and "the romance-minded men rushed to polish themselves to pursue her favor."

During her years as a Daoist priestess, Yu Xuanji exchanged poems and letters with famous poets and ministers in the central government such as Li Ying and the instructor of the Directorate of Education, Wen Tingyun. As evident through her poems in our collection, Yu Xuanji also took the initiative to pursue her own love interests and actively amplified the Tang popular imagination that saw exquisite Daoist priestesses as akin to demigoddesses.

Unfortunately, being seen as an embodiment of Immortals did not serve Yu Xuanji fully. She was executed at about the age of twenty-five as the result of a sensational murder case where Yu was accused of killing a maid. Even in the record of her contemporaries, the murder Yu was accused of was filled with mystery. For example, it was reported that the victim's body "looked alive" when it was discovered by Yu's enemies months after the supposed murder. The other conundrum of Yu Xuanji's violent demise came from her trial's ruling. Historical records indicate that masters or superiors who killed their maids during the Tang era rarely received capital punishment. Specifically, the *Tang Legal Code for Buddhist and Daoist Clergy* stated that such murders were punishable by one year of exile, not public execution. Despite these Tang customs and the fact that many aristocrats in the imperial court spoke up in her defense, Yu Xuanji met her end, laden with enigmas, in the autumn of 868 c.e..

Sadly, Yu Xuanji's unfortunate defamation did not end with her trial and death. Branding her posthumously as a courtesan, a social position lower even than the concubine status of a second wife, the orthodox Confucian scholars twisted interpretations of her poetry so that her writing was considered pornographic evidence of her seductive nature. Nonetheless, Yu Xuanji has continued to inspire others to this day. She appears in fiction by Mori Ogai (1862–1922 c.e.) and Robert van Gulik (1910–1967 c.e.), and countless movies, TV series, and musicals about her continue to captivate today's Chinese-speaking audiences.

神女天籟

Daoism and Goddess Culture

題隱霧亭

POEM FOR HERMIT FOG PAVILION

During the Tang Dynasty, Daoist priestesses revered the Immortals and goddesses, and they were even considered embodiments of various goddesses. It was not uncommon for laypeople to refer to a Daoist priestess as a goddess. The unadorned simplicity of this poem reveals Yu Xuanji's feeling of intimacy with the freedom of the Immortals, and her aspiration to join them even as she sleeps and dreams, facing the mountain peaks where the goddesses and Immortals reside. Yu expresses the comforting sense of purity and relief she finds through such devotion.

Spring flowers and autumn moons
enter my poems—
I live beneath the white sun
    and pure, clear nights
free as an Immortal.

With my pearl-drop screen
still unrolled,

I simply move my bed
    to sleep
facing the mountain peaks.

春花秋月入詩篇，白日清宵是散仙。
空捲珠簾不曾下，長移一榻對山眠。

送別

FAREWELL

While water and clouds are traditional Chinese poetic symbols of romantic and sensual love, Daoism adds the qualities of kindness, nourishment, and freedom. It's worth noting that the double symbolism may not be coincidental. As the poem begins, Yu Xuanji sets the tone for the flexible nature of both the imagery and the practitioner's mind by pointing to the flexible nature of water. This imagistic conceit first appears in chapter 18 of the Dao De Jing as an expression of a common Daoist ideal. Later on, it became an expression of the flexible nature of accomplished Daoists. Likewise, in Chinese culture, Mandarin ducks—especially when in a pair or a flock—are symbols of love in the intimate relationship of marriage. In a poetic move that Yu tends to employ in order to combine spiritual and romantic content, resulting in what may be considered her spiritual love poems, "Farewell" concludes with an image that would be particularly poignant at the time of its composition.

Flexible, without its own form,
    water settles into what holds it.
Clouds arise from no-mind,
    but they are willing to return.
Spring winds spread melancholy
    over the river as the sun descends—
separated from her companions,
    a wild duck flies alone.

水柔逐器知難定，雲出無心肯再歸。
惆悵春風楚江暮，鴛鴦一隻失群飛。

送別二

FAREWELL II

The story behind this poem is significant for Daoists as one of the earliest mentions of a historical human becoming immortal through practice. It is also vital for the goddess culture and its traditions. Qin Pavilion alludes to the legend of Nongyu, the talented, beautiful, and youngest daughter of King Mu of Qin. She was also an expert in *xiao*, an instrument modeled after the wings of a phoenix. King Mu built an elaborate palace on a high tower for this beloved daughter, where she lived and practiced. It is said that a male Immortal named Xiao Shi was so moved by her exquisite music that one day he suddenly appeared in her chamber. Not long after, they were married, and he taught her the art of immortality and celestial music inspired by the songs of the phoenix. As time passed and Nongyu's practice matured, Xiao Shi summoned two phoenixes, a male and a female. The couple flew away on the backs of the mythological birds to the land of Immortals, where their happiness knew no end. While the legend certainly inspired spiritual practice, in the lives of the poet and other women, relationships did not necessarily work out so well.

A few nights at Qin Pavilion satisfied my heart's request,
though I was surprised to see my immortal lover depart.
Let me just sleep and not talk about where the cloud has gone,
like a wild moth battering a burnt-out lamp.

秦樓幾夜愜心期，不料仙郎有別離。
睡覺莫言雲去處，殘燈一盞野蛾飛。

賦得江邊柳

POEM FOR A RIVER WILLOW

The sometime shadowed and weary feelings Yu endured in her difficult life can be found in this poem that nonetheless incorporates the erotic imagery important to the Daoist goddess culture. The highly valued flexibility Yu expressed with regard to water in her poem "Farewell" is also found in the nature of the willow tree and in what was required of women at this time. Yu's ability to express the complex lives of female spiritual practitioners is quite apparent as she weaves the images of this poem together.

Jade green along a desolate shore,
    smoky figures enter a distant house—
with their shadows spread out on autumn waters,
    fading blossoms lure other guests.

Old roots hidden in a fish den,
    low-hanging vines entangling a visitor's skiff—
on such a bleak night of wind and rain,
    waking from a dream only adds more sorrow.

翠色連荒岸，烟姿入遠樓。
影鋪秋水面，花落釣人頭。
根老藏魚窟，枝低繫客舟。
瀟瀟風雨夜，驚夢復添愁。

酬李郢夏日釣魚回見示

RESPONSE TO LI YING'S INVITATION TO GO FISHING ON A SUMMER DAY

In this spirited poem, Yu employs witty terms and spiritual imagery for the commonplace purpose of turning down a neighbor's invitation to go fishing. The neighbor may not have been one Yu favored, but it is also possible that she was just playing hard to get. The fragrant osmanthus branches found in the poem often allude to achievements and fertility, but its appearance here is likely literal. Possibly, the neighbor gave the poet a gift of osmanthus to hint at his other intentions. As a free-spirited woman, however, Yu alludes to Dao and Zen here, but only to express rejection. Perhaps the neighbor's poetic invitation referred to them as an enticement to draw the poet out, but Yu is nothing if not wise, and she returns the names of his enticement to indicate that she can see through his wiles.

Though we live in the same lane,
year after year our paths don't cross.
Casual conversation may soften an older woman,
while fragrant osmanthus bends the fresh boughs,
but the Dao's essence dupes both ice and snow,
and Zen mind just laughs at finery and silk.
Although traces of you have climbed clear to the Milky Way,
there's still no pathway to me through the mist and waves.

住處雖同巷，經年不一過。
清詞勸舊女，香桂折新柯。
道性欺冰雪，禪心笑綺羅。
跡登霄漢上，無路接烟波。

導懷

EMBODIED

Yu expresses the pure and joyful experience of her fully embodied being, exactly as the woman she is, in this poem where the embodiment of outer and inner worlds as one is as natural as clear water in a stream. While practitioners know the Dao cannot truly be named, the times when it may be experienced are treasured.

Free and at ease,
　　　with my body peaceful and calm,
　　　I flow through this landscape alone.
When the moon breaks through the scattering clouds
　　　and floats in the river,
　　　I untie my boat and drift out to sea.
I will play my harp in Emperor Wu's temple
　　　and recite my poems at Marquess Yu's estate.
　　　Bamboos in a grove might be my companions,
and bits of pebble can make really good friends.
　　　Let the finches squabble for position in vain,
　　　gold and silver hold no interest for me.

I fill my wine cup with the greenness of spring,
    plucking songs of seclusion for the moonlit night.
    Surrounding my stone walkway is a pure, quiet pond—
I remove my hairpin to reflect its delicate streams.
    Lying in bed with my books all around me,
    I get up half-drunk to run a comb through my hair.

閑散身無事，風光獨自游。
斷雲江上月，解纜海中舟。
琴弄蕭梁寺，詩吟庾亮樓。
叢篁堪作伴，片石好爲儔。
燕雀徒爲貴，金銀志不求。
滿杯春酒綠，對月夜琴幽。
遠砌澄清沼，抽簪映細流。
臥床書冊遍，半醉起梳頭。

訪趙鍊師不遇

VISITING ALCHEMY MASTER ZHAO,
WITHOUT LUCK

Where are you with your immortal companions,
your dark-robed assistant left alone at your home?
Your stove still warms the elixir,
tea leaves cook in your yard.
With the lamp light dim on your ornate walls,
and the sun slanting shadows on your banner poles,
I look back with deep regard—
flowering branches hang over your walls.

何處同仙侶，青衣獨在家。
暖爐留煮藥，鄰院爲煎茶。
畫壁燈光暗，幡竿日影斜。
殷勤重回首，墙外數枝花。

夏日山居

SUMMER IN THE MOUNTAIN

Yu Xuanji was deeply versed in the history of Chinese and Daoist legend, myth, and literature. This was true for all our poets. When she spreads her garments on the yard's small tree in the third line, she is alluding to a story about Ruan Ji, an artistic and early Daoist inspiration. One day, Ruan's rich cousins were hanging expensive garments in their front courtyard to dry and ward off mildew. As Ruan didn't have any delicate clothes, he simply laid on his back in his front yard and exposed his belly in the sun. His family was shocked when they saw this, so they asked, "What are you doing?" Hearing their tone, Ruan didn't budge, but simply replied, "I'm sunning the books in my belly so they don't grow mildew." While Yu refers to "the hidden path" in the poem and often compares her female narrators or protagonists to male cultural icons, as she does here, the lighthearted spirit of Ruan can be felt throughout, culminating with the light breeze that Yu trusts will always circle her back around.

I moved my immortal quarters to this place,
where shrubs blossom everywhere without being sown.
Spreading out my garments on the yard's small tree,
I sit above the fresh spring and float cups of wine.
From my balcony railings, there's a hidden path through
　　deep bamboo.
Fine woven silks embrace my messy pile of books.
Freely, I ride a painted boat and sing to the shining moon,
trusting the light breeze will circle me back around.

移得仙居此地來，花叢自遍不曾栽。
庭前亞樹張衣桁，坐上新泉泛酒杯。
軒檻暗傳深竹徑，綺羅長擁亂書堆。
閑乘畫舫吟明月，信任輕風吹却回。

愁思

CONTEMPLATING MELANCHOLY

A shower of leaves floats to the ground in the gentle evening rain,
    while I caress vermillion strings and sing quietly to myself.
Plunged deeply in what I feel, I don't regret not having
    true companions—
cultivating essence, I vainly try to leave all waves
    of suffering behind.
The sound of my elders' carriage is clear outside my gate,
    many Daoist books pile up by my pillow.
Despite my common cloth robe, eventually I will live
    in the heavenly realm,
where green waters and blue mountains
    pass by from time to time.

落葉紛紛暮雨和，朱絲獨撫自清歌。
放情休恨無心友，養性空拋苦海波。
長者車音門外有，道家書卷枕前多。
布衣終作雲霄客，綠水青山時一過。

暮春即事

NOTES OF LATE SPRING

Living in a dark alley behind shambled gates,
I have few companions or friends—
my perfect lover boy only stays on in my dreams.
So whose banquet with fine silks
floats out this fragrant incense,
and what pavilion releases such singing to the wind?
Living just beside the street, the noise of martial drums
shocked me out of my morning sleep.
The screech of magpies in my unused yard
churns up the youthful restlessness I feel.
How can I keep chasing such worldly things
when I know this body
is the same as an untied boat?

深巷窮門少侶儔，阮郎唯有夢中留。
香飄羅綺誰家席，風送歌聲何處樓。
街近鼓聲喧曉睡，庭閑鵲語亂春愁。
安能追逐人間事，萬里身同不繫舟。

感懷寄人

A LETTER TO EMBODY FEELINGS

Like the well-loved thirteenth-century Persian poet Rumi, Yu Xuan-ji's poems often braid together the imagery and longing found in the spiritual and sensual worlds. Rumi referred to his "Beloved Friend," and in like fashion, Yu waits in this poem for her inner-most friend. It is a mark of Yu's insight and talent to have incorporated this poetic conceit at such a young age, but her invention goes deeper still, since she draws images that were traditionally associated with the masculine (*yang*) principle into the *yin* world of a woman's life and sexuality. Peach and plum blossoms are two such images, as are pine, devilwood, and bamboo, which symbolize the Confucian moral ideals of reputable lords. In turning things around as she has and overtly expressing her woman's longing for a soulmate with whom she looks forward to sharing sexual intimacy, Yu is clear that her fragrant orchid's mind (a traditional symbol for solitude, inner purity, and spiritual integrity) is in no way diminished or disturbed. After all, as a practicing Daoist, she understands that the active *yang* principle found throughout the natural world is found in women, too.

I give voice to my anguish with vermillion strings—
the depth of my feelings just can't be held back.
Looking forward to the intimacy of clouds and rain
does not arouse my fragrant orchid's mind.
Peach and plum blossoms are radiant,
nothing can block the pursuit of my excellent lord—
indigo pines and devilwood
still long to be admired by the crowd.
My moss-covered stairs are pure in the moonlight,
this poet's voice rises from bamboo grasses deep in my yard.
In front of my gate, red leaves spread out on the ground,
I will leave them untouched, waiting for my innermost friend.

恨寄朱弦上，含情意不任。
早知雲雨會，未起蕙蘭心。
灼灼桃兼李，無妨國士尋。
蒼蒼松與桂，仍羨世人欽。
月色苔堦淨，歌聲竹院深。
門前紅葉地，不掃待知音。

女權初覺

Female Identity

遊崇真觀南樓睹新及第題名處

TOURING THE SOUTH HALL OF CHONGZHEN DAOIST TEMPLE AND READING THE WORKS OF THE NEW MINISTERS

In this poem, we see one of the great pains of Yu Xuanji's life—the inability, due to her gender, to take the national exam whose subject was poetry, whereby she might try to receive the kind of official recognition for her poetic talent that would allow her to advance in the social and economic realms. Such advancement was no simple matter of an egoic desire on her part. Since Yu came from a commoner background, she was relegated to the position of her husband's "lesser wife," a low social standing akin to what might be thought of as a sex slave. Besides, her husband's primary and aristocratic wife was known to physically abuse Yu as well. The "brutal hooks" to which she refers are both the literal ideographs in the poems written by the male honorees, whose names were listed publicly on a tablet for all to see, and society's restrictions that Yu bitterly railed against.

Cloud peaks fill my eyes, banishing the light of spring—
clear, brutal hooks form beneath their fingers!
I hate that my poems must hide beneath my woman's robes—
I lift my head in vain and envy the names of their honorees.

雲峰滿目放春晴，歷歷銀鈎指下生。
自恨羅衣掩詩句，舉頭空羨榜中名。

江行

RIVER TRAVEL

While there are many famous poems about pleasurable travel
by male poets in Chinese literature, travel for leisure by women
was almost unheard of in the Tang period. Nonetheless, Yu Xu-
anji was the first female literary figure to address this theme,
and she has quite a few travel poems with geographical ref-
erences in her work, some of which serve as critiques of this
social restriction against women. For example, in the first two
lines of this poem, Yu mimics the kinds of lines written re-
peatedly by male poets and may have chosen to mention Parrot
Island as part of her critique. It is important to note, however,
that traditional male critics took aim at her boldness and often
quoted the final lines of this poem (which include a reference
to the famous antirealist "butterfly dream" allegory by the
third-century B.C.E. Daoist philosopher Zhuangzi) as evidence
of Yu Xuanji's licentious nature.

Grand River hugs the sloping flank
    of Wuchang City,
with ten thousand households
    in front of Parrot Island.
Cruising on this painted boat,
    my morning sleep is just not long enough—
as a butterfly in my dream,
    I keep my eye out for flowers.

大江橫抱武昌斜，鸚鵡洲前萬戶家。
畫舸春眠朝未足，夢爲蝴蝶也尋花。

贈鄰女

TO THE GIRL NEXT DOOR

In classical Chinese romantic literature, women almost always appear as the heartbroken and abandoned lover. The strong-spirited Yu Xuanji gives us a good portrait of that cliché, but then she turns it on its head at the end of her poem with quite a unique move for the time: she reminds the young woman that while Wang Chang, the elusive and no doubt handsome man she desires, may not be obtainable, men like the legendarily handsome literary giant Song Yu (who we meet in Xue Tao's poem "Pilgrimage to the Temple of Wu Mountain," page 62) have far from disappeared.

Feeling shame in the daytime, you hide behind silk sleeves.
Anxious in spring, you have no energy to get up and dress.
It's easy to pursue a priceless treasure,
but impossible to find a faithful lover.
So you bury your face in your pillow
and let your tears stream down,
or conceal yourself among flowers
as your heart quietly breaks.
Since you still can catch a glimpse of men like Song Yu,
why keep resenting the elusive Wang Chang?

羞日遮羅袖，愁春懶起妝。
易求無價寶，難得有心郎。
枕上潛垂淚，花間暗斷腸。
自能窺宋玉，何必恨王昌。

賣殘牡丹

UNSOLD PEONY

In a society that so clearly favored the male—the *yang,* or masculine, principle in Daoist terms—it was no small thing for a young woman to know and believe in her value, talents, and spiritual depth. While Yu Xuanji certainly longed for the companionship of a lover, she also understood that despite what she was unable to achieve because of societal restrictions, her talent and spiritual aspirations were not to be taken lightly by anyone, and especially by herself. It may be that in this poem she is putting up a bit of a brave front, so to speak, but the poem reveals far more than that.

> Facing into the wind, you sigh for the flurry of falling blossoms,
> their fragrant essence fading in yet another passing spring.
> But your own high price keeps many from inquiring,
> while your deep fragrance prevents butterflies from drawing
>   near.
> Your red blossoms are fit to live only in the palace—
> how can your jade leaves be soiled by the dusty road?

By the time you move on to the celestial garden,
ordinary men will regret losing their chance to procure.

臨風興歎落花頻，芳意潛消又一春。
應爲價高人不問，卻緣香甚蝶難親。
紅英只稱生宮裏，翠葉那堪染路塵。
及至移根上林苑，王孫方恨買無因。

心聲情韻

Love Poems

———————

江陵愁望寄子安

SORROWFUL POEM TO ZI'AN
FROM JIANGLIN COUNTY

Despite Yu Xuanji's devotion to the Daoist path that so influenced
her life and poetry, after her marriage to Li Zi'an dissolved, she
never let go of her feelings toward Zi'an, as her biography and
writing make clear.

Maple leaves
    on thousands of branches—
delayed, the boat sails hide
    behind the bridge as the sun goes down.
My memory of you
    is like the Yangzi's waters—
flowing restlessly,
    day and night without end.

楓葉千枝復萬枝，江橋掩映暮帆遲。
憶君心似西江水，日夜東流無歇時。

春情寄子安

SPRING FEELINGS SENT TO ZI'AN

The mountain path is steep,
    the stony steps a danger,
but I don't worry about these hardships—
    my yearning is for you.
Ice melting in the far-off stream
    tenderly echoes your own pure sound.
The cold and distant snow peaks
    make me long for your noble disposition.
Please don't listen to profane songs
    or fall ill from springtime wine.
Resist the contagion of time-wasters,
    who indulge in late-night board games.
Unlike stones that shift around, our vow
    will be like long-lasting pines,
though flying together wing to wing,
    robe to robe, will surely take some time.

Even though I dislike traveling alone
    at winter's end,
I long to be together
    under spring's Fish Moon.
Far from you now,
    what would make a talisman that can endure?
My falling tears, the shining sun,
    this poem.

山路欹斜石磴危，不愁行苦苦相思。
冰銷遠澗憐清韻，雪遠寒峰想玉姿。
莫聽凡歌春病酒，休招閑客夜貪棋。
如松匪石盟長在，比翼連襟會肯遲。
雖恨獨行冬盡日，終期相見月圓時。
別君何物堪持贈，淚落晴光一首詩。

次韻西鄰新居兼乞酒

MATCHING POEM TO WESTERN NEIGHBOR'S NEW ESTATE AND BEGGING FOR WINE

A popular game in classical Chinese poetry involved writing poems that matched the subject and rhymes written by another poet-player of the game. We don't have the poem Yu Xuanji is matching, but Yu's response relies on her vast knowledge of Chinese myth and legend to strengthen her creation. For example, the third line subtly refers to a story about the legendarily handsome and talented Song Yu, who we meet in other poems by Yu and the other poets in this volume. In the next line, Yu brings to mind a widely known folk story where a lover or wife would climb to some high point in the mountains and, day after day, faithfully look in the direction of her beloved who may have gone off to war. She would do this with such devotion that in the end, she would become part of the outcropping, which Yu expresses as "a cliff of faith." Both the River of Stars and the Xiao-Xiang River appear in myths that involve the separation of lovers, and so Yu brings them into her poem to emphasize the longing she feels for her beloved companion from whom she has been separated far too long. It should be noted that given the emotional content in this poem, what Yu has written may not just be part of an innocent exchange among friends but her poetic reply to a poem originally sent by her lover.

Since your poem arrived, I've recited it a hundred times,
the feelings in each word so alive, echoing the sound of gold.
As you look west, I know you long to scale the wall between us—
gazing into the distance, how could my heart not become a
cliff of faith?
We have no reason to just stare across the River of Stars in vain
or let the Xiao-Xiang River shatter our music and dreams.
When the Cold Festival brings on our longing for home,
why would we drink the sage's refined liqueur alone?

一首詩來百度吟，新情字字又聲金。
西看已有登垣意，遠望能無化石心。
河漢期睮空極目，瀟湘夢斷罷調琴。
況逢寒節添鄉思，叔夜佳醪莫獨斟。

詩書往來

Poems in Correspondence

和新及第悼亡詩

ABOUT JOY AND LOSS

A branch of bay laurel
   blends in elegance with dark mist,
alongside rivers, ten thousand peach trees
   blossom red in the rain.

For now, let's get drunk with celebratory cups of wine
   and leave your sad gazing behind—
from ancient times until now,
   sorrow and joy have been just the same.

一枝月桂和烟秀，萬樹江桃帶雨紅。
且醉尊前休悵望，古來悲樂與今同。

冬夜寄飞卿

TO WEN TINGYUN
ON A WINTER'S NIGHT

Moments where Daoist practitioners are able to transcend life's demanding rigors may be rare, but Yu Xuanji reveals the depth of her practice in this poem where her solitary and often painful life nonetheless finds fulfillment. Wen Tingyun, a seminal poet in creating the new literary lyrical form of poetry in China, was Yu Xuanji's teacher and poetic mentor. In this poem, Yu draws together her life as a Daoist and her poetic talent in a lyrical statement that lets her mentor see that the promise of wholeness both practices can sometimes reveal is something she has come to know.

How unbearable, rummaging for poems
    to read aloud beneath my lamp
on this long sleepless night
    with my bedding so frightfully cold.
A bitter wind rises in my courtyard
    filled with twigs and leaves.

I peek through the silk curtains
    and pity the sinking moon.

Relaxed now, without restraint,
    my hopes have finally been fulfilled—
whether at its peak or in decline,
    in the emptiness I see original mind.
Living in seclusion, I don't just
    nest in the phoenix's tree—
as the sun goes down,
    chirping sparrows circle the woods in vain.

苦思搜詩燈下吟，不眠長夜怕寒衾。
滿庭木葉愁風起，透幌紗窗惜月沈。
疏散未閑終遂願，盛衰空見本來心。
幽棲莫定梧桐處，暮雀啾啾空繞林。

AFTERWORD
The World of the Poets

While the poems of Li Ye, Xue Tao, and Yu Xuanji are dynamic, fresh, and immediately relatable by readers today, it is remarkable and important to remember that these poets lived in another civilization more than one thousand years ago. The country, literary tradition, belief system, and social-gender structures in which the poets spent their lives were very different from what might be called "the here and now" of the twenty-first century. In order to somewhat round out an understanding of the poets and their poems, what follows is a very brief overview of the country and time in which they lived.

The Tang Dynasty was a mighty empire that ruled from 618 C.E. to 907 C.E., spanning much of the land we now know as China. This dynamic empire had its capital and political center in Chang'an, present-day Xi'an in northwestern China. Like today's China, it also had several economic and cultural centers in the south, such as the Chengdu area in the southwest and the Suzhou-Yangzhou region in its southeast. Trade routes connected Tang China to the rest of the ancient world, including the frequently traveled and well-known Silk Road that spans much of Eurasia, connecting Chang'an and Rome. New infrastructures, such as the Grand Canal waterway, were finished in the early seventh century and connected diverse regions of the empire, which allowed for the distribution of goods, wealth, and ideas within the country.⁴ The rulers and residents of the Tang Empire enjoyed a peaceful realm and economic prosperity for the first half of the empire's history, until the year 755 C.E. when An Lushan, a powerful general, rebelled against the crown. Although the rebellion was reined in after eight years, it significantly weakened the empire and fractured it into regional powers controlled by feuding warlords. Such conditions lasted and worsened for 144 years, until coups and commoner rebellions brought the Tang Dynasty to a bloody end in 907 C.E.

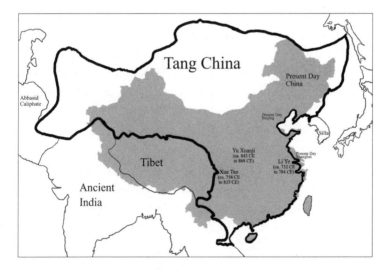

Map of Tang China's border compared to present-day China and where the poets lived for most of their lives.

Our poets' lives spanned the declining half of the Tang Dynasty. Li Ye was born around 732 C.E., and Yu Xuanji, born over one hundred years later, was executed at the age of twenty-five in 868 C.E. Civil unrest and the yearning to return to the glory and stability of the early Tang marked both the political reality and the cultural zeitgeist of the mid and late Tang Dynasty.

Poetry in Tang China

Poetry was one of the most significant accomplishments of the Tang Empire. The Chinese culture has long valued poems to represent the realm's cultural landscape, as well as the ability of poetry to bring moral education to all classes of the populace and the sophisticated way it meaningfully reflects the poets' inner world. As such, poetry was also respected as a candid representation of a poet's virtue, subconscious beliefs, and thinking, including the poet's ability to clarify, organize, and present ideas. The Tang Crown institutionalized this supportive sentiment in a national exam system for ministers and made poetry the subject of the exams. From commoner to high aristocracy, any male was eligible to participate in the national exams and potentially join the minister class after receiving a rank in the final test.[5] For example, Xue Tao's lover, Yuan Zhen, and Yu Xuanji's husband, Li Yi, both scored well in the exams.[6] The test and their standing, once the results were known, made them prized new members of the aristocracy, eligible to marry highborn women whose families would offer indispensable resources to their political careers.

One result of such an exam system was that poetry became the focus of education for the nation's best and brightest from a young age. It also meant that almost all issues of importance in Tang life were expressed and shared in poetry. Common topics ranged from romantic feelings and personal correspondence to reflections about social injustice and commentaries on international politics. It is no wonder that Chinese poetry reached one of its all-time peaks in the Tang Dynasty.

The three poets featured in this book were actively involved in the literary circles of their times, even though they were women. During the years shortly before and after the 755 C.E. An Lushan Rebellion, in Li Ye's lifetime, the four- and eight-lined regulated verses, respectively known as *jueju* and *lyushi*, developed significantly and reached their maturity.[7] This style, highly structured in tone, rhyme, and narrative arc, fills our current volume and dominates as one of the two main genres of Chinese poetry until the modern era. As a trailblazer in regulated verses, Li Ye created one of the finest early samples ever written, "Poem to Proofreader Elder Brother Seven" (page 42).

After a period of relative stagnation, the development of Chinese poetry picked up again during the lifetime of our second poet, Xue Tao, primarily due to the works of seminal poets such Bai Juyi and his colleague Yuan Zhen,[8] who enters the romantic narrative in our collection as one of Xue Tao's lovers and patrons. Yu Xuanji, our youngest poet, was active in literary circles when Chinese poetry embarked on its subsequent pivotal development, that of *ci*, or lyrical poems. Yu's mentor, Wen Tingyun, was often credited as the founder of the style—the evolution of which lasted beyond the then failing Tang Empire.[9] Scholars and academics often use the poems we translated here as firsthand material when studying the Tang Dynasty, especially regarding women and religion.[10]

Tang and Pre-Tang Daoism

Daoism was the Tang Dynasty's ruling clan's faith because the imperial family shared their last name with Lao Zi, the author of the Dao De Jing and one of the first Daoist philosophers.[11] Significantly different from its contemporary form, the Daoist religion leading up to and during the Tang Dynasty was steeped in alchemy, naturalism, romantic mysteries, and colorful rituals, some of an erotic nature.[12]

The wealth of spiritual traditions that Daoism, Confucianism, and classical Chinese literature commonly drew upon were established well before Daoism's institutionalization. In *Making Transcendents*, Robert Campany explained that this spiritual heritage existed as a "loosely cohesive tradition [and] a body of ideas and practices that had its main elements already in place by the late third century B.C.E. and was well established by the turn of the first millennium."[13] In the *Abbreviated Dictionary of Daoism*, Huang Haide explains that one of the origins of this system of ideas and practices is the Chinese Bronze Age divination practice *Wu Zhu*— the details of which are mostly lost.[14] Wu Zhu was more than just inspiration for our poets and other literary figures; women were active practitioners. Evidence of a number of the divinations were recorded as early as the oracle bones ca. 1250 B.C.E.[15] The diviners took on prominent roles, especially in the Chu culture. The extent of Chu culture's influence is still under archaeological and scholarly reconstruction, but a fifth-century B.C.E. history text, *Talk of Nations*, described in its "Talk of Chu" chapter that the female diviners were called *wu*,[16] after whom the tradition was named. *Explanation of Texts*, the second-century C.E. Chinese dictionary, further elucidated that "Wu were female diviners who served the formless and brought the gods down [to the human realm] through dance."[17]

"Talk of Chu" explained that these diviners "embodied other-worldly physical beauty and often served as the advisors of kings. Their sagaciousness could enlighten the distant realms, and they were learned in rituals, geography, history, and literature." Scholars trust the *Songs of Chu*, a collection of ritual poetry from the kingdom of Chu (ca. 1030–223 B.C.E.), as firsthand material when studying the Wu Zhu divination belief system. The text is coauthored by Song Yu, our poets' spiritual hero and romantic idol. The records of Wu Zhu divinations as living practices went as late as the late third century C.E.,[18] when Daoism began to transform into organized religion.

In addition to the Wu Zhu divination practice, Tang Daoism and our poets also drew heavily on the goddess mythologies in the Chinese spiritual tradition. The matriarch of the tradition's dynamic goddess pantheon was the Western Queen Mother, the divine bestower of elixirs and guru of transcendental practices who lived in the Celestial Palace in Kunlun Mountain.[19] She and her assistants, Mystic Woman and Unsullied Woman, taught the Yellow Emperor (one of the five mythological emperors of China from prehistoric times) the science and art of immortality after he established a sagacious rule on earth and founded the ancestral lineage to which over 90 percent of contemporary Chinese people trace their roots.

Another favorite of our poets and Chinese literature is Princess Yao, the goddess of erotic passion and affairs. The goddess was the daughter of Fiery Emperor, who invented agriculture and herbal medicine. As mentioned on page 55, Princess Yao was always a free-spirited and passionate girl but accidentally drowned while playing near Wu Gorge. From then on, she took the form of the gorge's clouds and transformed at will into a beautiful maiden to court and seduce men who suited her fancy.[20] The Daoist feminine pantheon had countless other goddesses, such as Moon Goddess Chang-eh, Star Goddess Weaver Maiden, and Sun Goddess Xi He, just to name a few. Ordinary people could encounter them through fortunate accidents or Daoist practices such as qigong, fasting, meditation, ritual baths, making and consuming alchemical elixirs, and so on. Like Princess Nongyu of the Phoenix Pavilion, whose legend influenced poems by Li Ye and Yu Xuanji, mortal women could also become goddesses through practicing the Dao.[21]

The awareness of physicality in the legends of Daoist goddesses was no accident, as erotic rituals formed a part of the historical Daoist practices, leading up to at least the Tang Dynasty. Written records for related practices existed as the Dao of Yin by at least the early second century in the "Yi Wen Records" in the *Book of Han*.[22] The ancient Chinese language often used euphemism and talked about these erotic practices as the Art of Bedchambers or the Science of Yin-Yang. The *Book of Han* recorded eight schools of such arts with 186 volumes of texts. It also stated that "the Art of Bedchambers were the pinnacles of emotional essence and the moments for the supreme Dao." The fourth-century Daoist Ge Hong went into detail in his seminal practice manual, *Baopuzi*.[23]

Ge Hong taught that "the practitioners of qigong and [Daoist] meditation should also know the Art of Bedchambers. How come? Not knowing the Science of Yin-Yang, [the practitioners] would often become tired and tarnished. It would be difficult for them to get a hold of their *qi*'s movement." Other chapters of *Baopuzi* further elucidate that "not knowing the Art of Bedchambers, even taking thousands of kinds of elixir . . . will not help." It also says, "Among the ten or so lineages of the Art of Bedchambers, some practice it as first aid, and some employ it as medicine. Some [schools] take the women's essence to benefit the men, while some others use [the art] for longevity. The main principle is in the one exercise of returning the discharges to the brain."

These erotic rituals were in practice until at least the early Tang Dynasty. The renowned seventh-century Daoist and medical doctor Sun Simiao went into graphic detail in volume 83, chapter 8, of his celebrated medical text *Essential Priceless Prescription for All Urgent Ills.*[24] Professor Jia Jinhua concludes in *Gender, Power, and Talent* that the Tang Daoist tradition "had its sexual practice as a way to attain longevity and immortality."[25] Toward the end of the Tang Dynasty, however, which coincided with the lifetime of Yu Xuanji in the mid to late ninth century, it became increasingly hazy as to how widespread such erotic rituals remained in mainstream Daoism. In the early tenth century, Du Guangting detailed the life and practice of ten Daoist women in his *Records of Collected Immortals in The Celestial City,*[26] finishing only a few decades after Yu Xuanji's demise. The text did not mention erotic rituals but instead emphasized fasting, alchemical elixirs, asceticism, and celibacy. After that, the celibate Daoist Quanzhen order was founded in the mid-twelfth century and gained popularity lasting until the present day.

While we cannot ignore these developments, we also cannot view them as conclusive evidence that the Daoist erotic ritual went out of practice, since we know many twenty-first-century Chinese medicine professionals still use treatments detailed in Sun Simiao's *Essential Priceless Prescription for All Urgent Ills.* An alternative possibility was that the practitioners became increasingly private after the Tang Dynasty, and new instructions were unnecessary.

Daoist Priestesses and Tang Women

Compared to China in other historical periods, the early Tang society placed more value on the power of femininity,[27] and about twenty-eight imperial princesses were ordained into Daoist institutions.[28] As a result, the Daoist priestesses enjoyed greater respect and social freedom than other classical Chinese women. The Tang Daoist priestesses gave public sermons, performed rituals, traveled freely, and became religious mentors even to emperors. The popular Tang erotic goddess culture also extended to include Daoist priestesses. Their romantic lives were publicly celebrated, and the community respectfully referred to them as "female Immortals" or by the honorific term, "semi-goddesses."[29]

The Tang Daoist religion amplified the feminine voice in the Wu Zhu divination tradition, the goddess pantheon, and the erotic practices, all of which provided important literary inspiration and social capital for the three celebrated poets in our collection. We have included many verses that romanticize and allude to the divine union, euphemized as clouds and rain, between ancestral shaman kings of Chu and the immortal Goddess of Wu Mountain.[30]

As mentioned in our preface, Li Ye and Yu Xuanji were ordained Daoist priestesses. In Tang China, this meant that they were respected as spiritual equals of their male counterparts and could be active in public spheres.[31] Socially and institutionally empowered, Li Ye and Yu Xuanji went further with their goddess inspirations. Li actively embodied the transcendental sexuality of the goddesses when relating to her lovers. Her poem "Departing on a Moonlit Night" (page 9) relies on the legend of a seduction between the Yellow Emperor and the Western Queen Mother who made the Celestial Palace her home.

Li also openly expressed her physical experiences and desires in one poem as "a raging wind, holding back thunder, / or the low moan of a river that cannot flow" (page 14). In another she writes, "Above the railing of a hundred-foot well, / peach branches have already budded red" (page 33).

Almost a century later, Yu Xuanji leveraged the same body of literary and transcendental traditions to pursue spiritual and marital independence. Sadly, despite her evident talent, Yu's short life was brought to a violent end.

However, her Daoist practices and the goddess tradition "empowered her to poetically transform herself from an impoverished, marginalized, and oppressed commoner woman into an Immortal."[32] In this altered universe, she expressed being free "as an untied boat" (page 115) and declared that she "will live in the heavenly realm, / where green waters and blue mountains pass by from time to time" (page 114).

Yu Xuanji was also skilled in embodying the Daoist goddess pantheon to empower herself in her day-to-day interactions, often with male suitors. In one verse, she boasted, "Although traces of you have climbed clear to the Milky Way, / there's still no pathway to me through the mist and waves" (page 108). And in another of her untamed, spirited poems ("A Letter to Embody Feelings," page 116), she embodied the tree goddesses and seductively wrote:

My moss-covered stairs are pure in the moonlight,
this poet's voice rises from bamboo grasses deep in my yard.
In front of my gate, red leaves spread out on the ground,
I will leave them untouched, waiting for my innermost friend.

Synthesizing the social-religious background of Tang Daoism and the evidence of erotic rituals with the emotions, lifestyle, and spirituality expressed by Tang Daoist priestesses in their own words, we might even begin to get hints that our poetic priestesses operated in polyamorous communities, just like the Daoist courtesan Xue Tao. Yet we must remain cautious about such speculation despite its allure. Any serious scholar will admit that it is excruciatingly difficult to pin down the exact dates of texts from over a millennium ago—especially considering romantic passion and relationships can change in a matter of a year or even a few months.

The three poets in our collection were unlikely to be norms for Tang women. As ordained Daoist clergy, Li Ye and Yu Xuanji were considered to have left the household life. They lived in convents with independent economies and were governed under a separate legal system as detailed by the *Tang Legal Code for Buddhist and Daoist Clergy*.[33] Xue Tao, being a member of the courtesan and entertainer caste, lived with severe social restrictions and suffered more institutional oppression than even manual and household slaves.[34] In short, the authors of our collection all lived and operated in the margins of their society.

Historical texts suggest that Tang women at large enjoyed more respect and independence compared to Chinese women from other historical periods. For example, the ability of Tang women to divorce and remarry, or to have lovers, as mentioned in our preface, was extraordinary at the time, as was their access to education and their ability to function as unique persons in societal fields otherwise restricted to men. But these freedoms were not able to be sustained.

The classical golden period for Chinese women came to a halt with the end of the Tang Dynasty when Chinese culture was turned to closely follow the patriarchy required by Confucianism. Li Ye, Xue Tao, and Yu Xuanji's legacies and their poems came under revisionist interpretations by orthodox Confucian scholars for the centuries that followed. These literary men viewed the poets' spirituality and independence as sins. In their writings, they cast the priestesses as prostitutes[35] and presented these female prodigies as counter-ideals to Confucian ethical society. The traditional Confucian scholars twisted the primary value of the poems in this collection and offered them as proof of their writers' licentious nature.[36] However, new archaeological findings from sites such as Dunhuang present us with materials that meaningfully challenge the orthodox critics' patriarchal interpretations of these poems.

The era of the three Daoist poets, and even that of their orthodox Confucian critics, are now long past. Yet the poetry left behind by these Tang spiritual women, infused with naturalism and romanticism, still uplifts and inspires across languages and civilizations until this day. Yu Xuanji summed it up well in "About Joy and Loss" when she wrote, "From ancient times until now, sorrow and joy have been just the same" (page 139).

NOTES ON THE POEMS

Notes Related to Li Ye's Poems

DEPARTING ON A MOONLIT NIGHT, page 9

Clouds and water symbolize sensual passion, lovemaking, and reproduction in Chinese literature.

A SONG TO THE SPRING OF THREE GORGES, page 13

"The flowing spring" refers to both a babbling brook in Wu Mountain and a solo piece played on the Chinese harp.

"Flat sand" subtly alludes to another significant Chinese harp composition. In addition to music, flat sand often appears as imagery in classical Chinese literature and art.

Lord Ruan, Ruan Ji (210–263 C.E.), was a famous early Daoist and master musician.

Zhong Rong is the courtesy name for Ruan Xian, Ruan Ji's nephew. He was also a renowned musician and early Daoist.

FEELINGS ARISE, page 16

"Melody of Phoenix Pavilion" alludes to two love stories in addition to the mythology we detailed in the poem's introduction. The first story below is so important to these Daoist poets that it also appears in the introduction to Yu Xuanji's poem, "Farewell II."

This story comes from 620 B.C.E., during the Spring and Autumn period. King Mu of Qin's youngest daughter, Nongyu, was talented and beautiful. She was an expert in *xiao*, a musical instrument modeled after the wings of a phoenix. King Mu built an elaborate palace on a high tower for Nongyu, where she lived and practiced. Her music was so exquisite that one day a male Immortal named Xiao Shi was moved by it and appeared in her chamber. They married, and he taught her the art of immortality and celestial music inspired by the songs of the phoenix. When Nongyu's practice matured, Xiao Shi summoned two phoenixes, a male and a female. The couple flew away on the backs of the mythological birds to the land of Immortals, where they lived happily ever after.

In addition to its apparent romance, this story is significant for Daoists because it is one of the earliest mentions of a historical human becoming immortal through practicing the Dao. It is also vital for the goddess culture and its traditions, so readers will see references to it repeatedly in our work.

The second love story was about Sima Xiangru (ca. 179–117 B.C.E.), a renowned musician and poet. Despite an early career that earned him fame in literature, Sima was still broke and lived in a state of near poverty after returning to his hometown. His fortunes improved when he was taken on as a protégé of Wang Ji, the magistrate of Linqiong. Wang introduced Sima to Zhuo Wangsun, a wealthy iron manufacturer. Sima immediately fell in love with Zhuo's recently widowed daughter, Zhuo Wenjun, also a famous musician, and pursued her by playing *Melody of Phoenix Pavilion*. She accepted his advances, but her father disagreed with their union, which led Sima and Zhuo Wenjun to elope. Sima's biography states that the couple supported themselves by running an ale shop until Wenjun's father was forced by public shame into recognizing their marriage. He gave the couple one million copper coins, one hundred servants, and other valuables from the dowry of Zhuo's first marriage.

WILLOW, page 20

"The east wind" is the spring wind. Most of China is in the monsoon belt, where the east wind brings rain from the Pacific Ocean in the east every year.

"The exiled hermit" alludes to Qu Yuan, a third-century B.C.E. poet who was exiled for his political views. In the Chinese poetic tradition, the narrators call themselves exiled hermits to show solidarity with staying true to one's nonmainstream values.

SENDING OFF YAN TO SHAN COUNTY, page 29

The Gate of Paradise is the western gate of Suzhou City. The western gate is also known as Chang Gate and has one gate for boat traffic and one for land traffic. The westward river from Chang Gate connects to the Grand Canal, which then connects an extensive network of waterways all over the country in Tang China.

The Wu Garden could be a physical location in Tang China or a metaphorical place. The rest of the poem includes many references to Suzhou City and Jiangsu Province, known as the Wu region, named after a pre-Confucian kingdom in the area.

SEEING OFF HAN KUI TO JIANGXI, page 40

Jiangxi Province and Suzhou, where Li Ye most probably lived, is connected by the Yangzi River.

Pen City is in present-day Ruichang City, near Qingpen Mountain.

Xiakou literally means "summer's opening." It was an independent city but is now a district in present-day Wuhan.

POEM TO PROOFREADER ELDER BROTHER SEVEN, page 42

Wucheng County is a place in Huzhou, Zhejiang Province.

"Yun Pavilion" refers to structures made of a type of wood called Rutaceae. Furniture made of Rutaceae can prevent book worms. Therefore, Rutaceae pavilions, halls, and desks refer to official scholars employed by the government.

Great Thunder is a lake in Wangjiang County of Anhui Province, a region to which Elder Brother Seven was traveling. It is also an allusion to "Letter to My Little Sister on the Shores of Great Thunder," a well-known poem from Bao Zhao (416–66 C.E.) to his sister, Bao Linghui, who was also a famous literary figure.

Notes Related to Xue Tao's Poems

PILGRIMAGE TO THE TEMPLE OF WU MOUNTAIN, page 62

Gaotang was the name of a Daoist temple in Wu Mountain. Legend says that it was built by Yao of Tang, one of the first mythological sage kings of China. A 2016 archaeological excavation revealed an over four-thousand-square-meter temple complex dating back to the Warring States period (475–221 B.C.E.). The temple complex was built on top of layers of burials influenced by Chu culture that had the legendarily handsome poet and diviner Song Yu as one of its cultural icons. Song Yu also wrote the "Ode of Gaotang" that describes the ritualized copulation between the Goddess of Wu Mountain and an ancestral king of Chu. King Qing, the historical Chu King referenced in this poem, had his full name as King Qing Xiang. The poet took the liberty to present him as King Xiang so that the original Chinese language flowed more poetically. Following the example in other works of Chinese literature, we now translate his name to King Qing for the same effect in the English poetry.

SENDING AN OLD-STYLE POEM TO WEIZHI, page 82

"Precious emerald jade" alludes to women from economically ordinary households.

TO ZHENG MEI ZHOU, page 88

Mei Zhou, Eyebrow County, is named after Mei Mountain, Eyebrow Mountain. This poem is dedicated to a minister with the last name Zheng, who worked at Mei Zhou in present-day Sichuan Province in southwestern China.

FAREWELL TO LI LANGZHONG, page 89

The Sichuan Alps, also known as Qin Ling, form a natural boundary between northern and southern China. It was on the way to wherever Li Langzhong was traveling.

In Chinese mythology, phoenixes only perch on parasol trees. When the parasol tree loses its flowers, the phoenixes must separate.

Notes Related to Yu Xuanji's Poems

SUMMER IN THE MOUNTAIN, page 112

"Float cups of wine" is a double allusion. One allusion refers to the Duke of Zhou (active ca. 1042 B.C.E.), a Confucian sage who floated wine cups on a spring day and wrote poems to celebrate the founding of Luo Yang. The other one references the sage of calligraphy, Wang Xizhi (303–61 C.E.). Wang wrote his best work for a gathering at Orchid Pavilion. During the occasion, the participants floated their wine cups in the spring and played poetry games.

CONTEMPLATING MELANCHOLY, page 114

"Common cloth robe" alludes to commoners because only ministers and aristocracy could wear silk robes in Tang China.

NOTES OF LATE SPRING, page 115

The screech of magpies is traditionally interpreted as an omen for good fortune.

TOURING THE SOUTH HALL OF CHONGZHEN DAOIST TEMPLE AND READING THE WORKS OF THE NEW MINISTERS, page 121

China's national exam system started in the Sui Dynasty (581–619 C.E.) and reached its final form in the Tang Dynasty (618–907 C.E.). It was customary for the government to give the scholars a parade while also publishing their names and works in a temporary shrine for public viewing and education. During the Tang Dynasty, the shrine was at Chongzhen Daoist Temple, and the subject of the exam was poetry.

RIVER TRAVEL, page 123

The geographical references in this poem are all about Wuhan, on the Yangzi River. Grand River is the Yangzi River, Wuchang City is now a district of Wuhan, and Parrot Island was a sandbar in the middle of the Yangzi River.

SPRING FEELINGS SENT TO ZI'AN, page 132

"Unlike stones that shift around" alludes to a poem about abandoned wives in the *Book of Songs*. The idea is that the rocks can turn, but the poet's heart is not like these rocks, so it does not turn back on vows of love.

ABOUT JOY AND LOSS, page 139

Bay laurel symbolizes scoring positions in the national exams, and peach blossoms are symbols of liveliness and good fortune.

TO WEN TINGYUN ON A WINTER'S NIGHT, page 140

"The phoenix's tree" alludes to the story of the phoenix in the Zhuangzi, where the mythical bird only perches on Chinese parasol trees.

NOTES

1. Gao, *Tang Women*, 7.
2. Liu, *Broad Stroke View of Tang Women's Life*, 7.
3. Ji, *Background Matters of Tang Poems*.
4. Lewis, *China's Cosmopolitan Empire*, 1–3.
5. Han, "Political Motivation in Empress Wu Ze-tian's Reform of Imperial Examination," *Journal of Nantong University*, 95–100.
6. Liu, "Imagery of Female Daoists in Tang and Song Poetry," 2–3.
7. Ge, *Poetry of the Tang & Sung Dynasty*, 99.
8. Ge, *Poetry of the Tang & Sung Dynasty*, 123–32.
9. Ge, *Poetry of the Tang & Sung Dynasty*, 170–73, 189–92.
10. Cahill, *Chinese Women's History Reader*, 137.
11. Jia, *Gender, Power, and Talent*, 2.
12. Bokenkamp, *Early Daoist Scriptures*, 10; Jia, *Gender, Power, and Talent*, 10.
13. Campany, *Making Transcendents*, xiii.
14. Huang and Li, *Abbreviated Dictionary of Daoism*, chap. 1.
15. Xueqin, "Xia-Shang-Zhou Chronology Project," *Journal of East Asian Archaeology*, 321–33.
16. Zuo, *Talk of Nations*, chap. "Talk of Chu," section 2.
17. Xu, *Explanation of Texts*, vol. 5, entry Wu.
18. Fang, *The Book of Jin*, vol. 94, chap. "Xiatong's Biography."
19. Campany, *Making Transcendents*, 37.

20. Zheng, ed., *Classics of Mountains and Seas*, 130. Note: The author and date of this most trusted and oldest collection of Chinese mythology is unknown.

21. Liu, *Collection of the Immortal's Biography:* chap. "Xiao Shi."

22. Ban, *Book of Han,* vol. "Yi Wen Records.". "Bed Chambers has eight schools with 186 volumes of texts. The Art of Bedchambers are the pinnacles of emotional essence and the moments for the supreme Dao. . . ."

23. Ge, *Baopuzi,* chap. 5 and chap. 8.

24. Sun, *Essential Priceless Prescription for All Urgent Ills,* vol. 83, chap. 8.

25. Jia, *Gender, Power, and Talent,* 10.

26. Du, *Records of Collected Immortals in the Celestial City.*

27. Jia, *Gender, Power, and Talent,* 11–12.

28. Jia, *Gender, Power, and Talent,* 18.

29. Jia, *Gender, Power, and Talent,* 16.

30. Cahill, *Chinese Women's History Reader,* 137.

31. Jia, *Gender, Power, and Talent,* 15.

32. Cahill, *Chinese Women's History Reader,* 136.

33. Jia, *Gender, Power, and Talent,* 3.

34. Gao, *Tang Women,* 63.

35. Liu, "Imagery of Female Daoists in Tang and Song Poetry," 5.

36. Jia, *Gender, Power, and Talent,* 164; and Chen, *The Collection of Three Tang Female Poets,* 184.

BIBLIOGRAPHY

Anonymous (ca. 420–589 C.E.). *Zhengtong Collection of Daoist Canon, Zhengyi Order: The Eight Unsullied True Essence Meditation and Visualization Instructions by the Grandest and Highest Dongzhen Immortal.* 正統道藏，正一部：洞真太上八素真精三景妙訣. Reprinted 1445.

Bai, Juyi (722–846 C.E.). *Bai Collection of Six Types of Documents.* Taipei: Taiwan shang wu yin shu guan, reprinted 1983.

Ban, Gu (32–92 C.E.). *Book of Han, Vol. Yi Wen Records.* 汉书：藝文志. Taipei: Jin xiu chu ban shi ye gu fen you xian gong si, reprinted 1993.

Bokenkamp, Stephen R. *Early Daoist Scriptures.* Berkeley: University of California Press, 1997.

Cahill, Suzanne. *The Chinese Women's History Reader.* Beijing: Beijing University Press, 2009.

Campany, Robert Ford. *Making Transcendents: Ascetics and Social Memory in Early Medieval China.* Honolulu: University of Hawai'i Press, 2009.

Chen, Dongyuan. *The History of Chinese Women's Daily Life.* 中国妇女生活史. Beijing: Commercial Press, 2017.

Collected poets (twelfth century–seventh century B.C.E.). *Book of Songs.* 詩經. Urumuqi: Xinjiang Teenagers Publishing House, reprinted 1999.

Du, Guangting (850–933 C.E.). *Records of Collected Immortals in The Celestial City.* 墉城集仙录. Ji'nan: Qi Lu Shu She, reprinted 1995.

Fang, Xuanling (579–648 C.E.). *The Book of Jin: Xiatong's Biography.* 晋书：夏统传. Taibei Shi: Jin xiu chu ban shi ye gu fen you xian gong si, reprinted 1993.

Gao, Shilian (?–647 C.E.). *Zhenguan Tabulation of Prominent Clans.* 贞观氏族志. Beijing: National Library of China's Collection of Archaeological Documents from Dunhuang.

Gao, Shiyu. *Tang Women.* Xi'an: Sanqin Publishing House, 1988.

Ge, Hong (284–364 C.E.). *Baopuzi.* 抱朴子. Changchun: Jinlin chu ban ji tuan you xian gong si, reprinted 2005.

Ge, Xiaoyin. *Poetry of the Tang & Sung Dynasty.* 唐詩宋詞的十五堂課. Gaoxiong: Wunan Publishing Ltd., 2007.

Han, Hong-Tao. "Political Motivation in Empress Wu Ze-tian's Reform of Imperial Examination." *Journal of Nantong University* 34, no. 1 (2018): 95–100.

Huang, Haide, and Gang Li. *The Abbreviated Dictionary of Daoism.* 簡明道教辭典. Chengdu: Sichuan University Press, 1991, chap. 1.

Huangfu, Mei (active 874–910 C.E.). *Short Tales of Three Waters.* 三水小牘. Shanghai: Shanghai gu ji chu ban she, reprinted 2002.

Ji, Yougong (active 1121–61 C.E.). *Background Matters of Tang Poems.* 女中诗豪. Shanghai: Shang wu yin shu guan, reprinted 1929.

———. *Background Matters of Tang Poems* vol. 2. 唐诗纪事：卷二. Shanghai: Shang wu yin shu guan, reprinted 1929.

Jia, Jinhua. *Gender, Power, and Talent: The Journey of Daoist Priestesses in Tang China.* New York: Columbia University Press, 2018.

Laozi (ca. 571 B.C.E.–?). *Dao De Jing* 道德經. Changchun: Jilin Wen Shi Chu Ban She, reprinted 2000.

Lewis, Mark Edward. *China's Cosmopolitan Empire: The Tang Dynasty.* Cambridge: Harvard University Press, 2012.

Li, Fang (925–996 C.E.), ed., et al. *Extensive Records of the Taiping Era.* 太平廣記. Shanghai: Shanghai gu ji chu ban she: Xin hua shu dian Shanghai fa xing suo fa xing, reprinted 1990.

Li, Xueqin. "The Xia-Shang-Zhou Chronology Project: Methodology and Results," *Journal of East Asian Archaeology* 4, no. 1 (2002): 321–33. doi. org/10.1163/156852302322454585.

Li, Ye, Xue Tao, and Yu Xuanji. *The Collection of Three Tang Female Poets.* 唐女诗人集三种. Edited by Wenhua Chen. Shanghai: Guji Publishing House, 1984.

Liu, Jianming. *Broad Stroke View of Tang Women's Life.* Hong Kong: Chinese University of Hong Kong, 2003.

Liu, Xiang (77 B.C.E.–6 C.E.). *A Collection of the Immortal's Biography.* 列仙传. Beijing: Beijing Ai ru sheng shu zi hua ji shu yan jiu zhong xin, digitized 2009.

Liu, Yang. "Imagery of Female Daoists in Tang and Song Poetry." PhD diss., University of British Columbia, 2011.

Liu, Yiqing (403–444 C.E.). *A New Account of the Tales of the World.* 世說新語. Beijing: Zhonghua Book Company, reprinted 2001.

Lu, Yu. "Readings of Chinese Poet Xue Tao." Master's thesis, University of Massachusetts Amherst, 2010.

Qu, Yuan (ca. 345–295 B.C.E.) and Yu Song (active 290–223 B.C.E.). *Song of Chu.* 楚辭. Changchun: Jilin Wen Shi Chu Ban She, reprinted 1999.

Song, Yu (active 290–223 B.C.E.). *Ode of Gaotang.* 高唐賦. Hong Kong: Guang zhi shu ju, reprinted 1950.

———. *Ode to the Goddess of Wu Mountain.* 神女賦. Hong Kong: Guang zhi shu ju, reprinted 1950.

Sun, Simiao (581–682 C.E.). *Essential Priceless Prescription for All Urgent Ills, Volume 83, Chapter 8.* 備急千金要方，卷八十三：八、房中补宜. Taipei: Taiwan shang wu yin shu guan, reprinted 1983.

Tanba, Yasuyori (912–95 C.E.). *Prescriptions to Treat the Heart, Vol. 28: Inner Chamber.* 医心方卷 28：房内. Tokyo: Haga Shoten, Shōwa, reprinted 1968.

Tang Imperial Government (ca. 637 C.E.). *Tang Legal Code for Buddhist and Daoist Clergy.*

Xin, Wenfang (ca. 1265–1325 C.E.). *Biographies of Tang Talents.* 唐才子传. Shanghai: Zhong Hua Shu Ju, reprinted 1965.

Xu, Shen (ca. 58–148 C.E.). *Explanation of Texts.* 说文. Changsha Shi: Yue ji shu she, reprinted 2006.

Xue, Tao (ca. 758–832 C.E.). *Xue Tao Shi Jian.* 薛涛诗笺. Beijing: Ren min wen xue chu ban she: Xin hua shu dian Beijing fa xing suo fa xing, reprinted 1983.

Zheng, Huisheng, ed. *The Classics of Mountains and Seas.* 山海经. Kaifeng: University of He'nan Press, reprinted 2008.

Zheng, Xianwen. *The Reconstruction and Research of Tang Legal Code for Buddhist and Daoist Clergy.* 唐代僧道格及其复原之研究. Beijing: China University of Political Science and Law, Department of Ancient Legal Text, 2004.

Zhong, Xing (1574–1625 C.E.), ed. *Collected Poems by Famous Women.* 名媛诗归. Ji'nan: Qi Lu shu she, reprinted 1997.

Zhuang, Zhou (ca. 369–286 B.C.E.). *Zhuangzi.* 莊子. Guangzhou: Hua Cheng Publications, reprinted 1998.

Zuo, Qiuming (active early 400s B.C.E.). *The Talk of Nations.* 国语. Beijing Shi: Zhonghua shu ju, reprinted 2007, chap. Talk of Chu.

ABOUT THE TRANSLATORS

PETER LEVITT's books of poetry, prose, and translation include *One Hundred Butterflies*, *Within Within*, *Fingerpainting on the Moon: Writing and Creativity as a Path to Freedom*, and his collaborative translations with Kazuaki Tanahashi, *The Complete Cold Mountain: Poems of the Legendary Hermit Hanshan*, *A Flock of Fools: Ancient Buddhist Tales of Wisdom and Laughter*, and *The Essential Dogen: Writings of the Great Zen Master*. In 1989, he received the Lannan Foundation Award in Poetry. He is the founding and guiding teacher of the Salt Spring Zen Circle in the lineage of Shunryu Suzuki Roshi. He lives on Salt Spring Island, British Columbia, with his wife, poet Shirley Graham.

REBECCA NIE is a Chinese American Zen master, scholar, and award-winning algorithm and new media artist. Born in China, she came of age in Canada and the United States. Rebecca Nie now serves as the Buddhist Chaplain-Affiliate at Stanford University. Chinese literature and cultural heritage are some of Nie's lifelong passions. She started writing Chinese poetry at the age of nine, studied the *Song of Chu* at ten, and by fifteen years old, she had memorized key passages from the Dao De Jing and the

Zhuangzi. Nie frequently published her prose and poetry in Chinese literary journals and was an assistant editor of Shenzhen Yucai Education Group's *Literary Extension Textbook Series.*

In Canada and the United States, Rebecca Nie continued her education in classical Chinese literature and Eastern spirituality while studying English. She published multiple times in professional English-language journals and magazines and graduated with honors from the University of Toronto and Stanford University. As a Zen master of the Korean Jogye Order and the founder of Mahavajra Seon Sanctuary, Rebecca Nie is dedicated to unleashing humanity's full potential through artistic expressions and offering systematic training in Eastern wisdom-spiritual traditions.

For scholarly resources or more information about the research that went into this book, contact Rebecca Nie directly at rnie@stanford.edu.